Praise for *Boyhood*

"Tremendously readable and powerful . . . a masterfully told, spare and accessible memoir."
—*The Boston Globe*

"Coetzee brings all the power of his craft to the evocation of his boyhood. In spare, controlled prose he takes us into his world."
—*Sunday Times*

"Astringent and grimly fascinating . . . Coetzee couches his remembrances in pithy urgent sentences from which emotion seems to explode."   —*Newsday*

"Mr. Coetzee writes, as always, with striking elegance. . . . Individual scenes are expertly, even beautifully, presented."
—*The Atlantic Monthly*

"The spare words of *Boyhood* are a liturgy of wisdom."
—*The Atlanta Journal-Constitution*

"This domestic drama is intensely painful and haunts the reader long after one has finished this short memoir."
—Caryl Phillips, *Bomb* magazine

"A powerful, disillusioned portrait of childhood and how, like South Africa, it encompasses both prelapsarian innocence and unconscionable violence." —*Kirkus Reviews*

"*Boyhood* presents the fears, contradictions, angers and sparse joys of his preteen childhood with a clarity, an innocence and a directness of a child."   —*Houston Chronicle*

"Affecting and effortlessly readable . . . *Boyhood* offers a rare glimpse into one writer's beginnings."
—*Detroit Free Press*

PENGUIN BOOKS

BOYHOOD

J. M. Coetzee was born in Cape Town, South Africa, in 1940
and educated in South Africa and the United States as a
computer scientist and linguist. His first work of fiction was
Dusklands. This was followed by *In the Heart of the Country*,
which won the premier South African literary award, the
CNA Prize; *Waiting for the Barbarians*, which was awarded
the CNA Prize, the Geoffrey Faber Memorial Prize, and the
James Tait Black Memorial Prize; *Life & Times of Michael K*,
which won the Booker Prize and the Prix Étranger Femina;
Foe; *Age of Iron*; and *The Master of Petersburg*, which won
The Irish Times International Fiction Prize. J. M. Coetzee
won the Jerusalem Prize in 1987. His other works include
translations, linguistic studies, and literary criticism.

To request Penguin Readers Guides by mail
(while supplies last),
please call (800) 778-6425 or write to:

Penguin Marketing, Dept. CC
Readers Guides Requests-B
375 Hudson Street
New York, NY 10014

J. M. COETZEE

BOYHOOD
Scenes from Provincial Life

PENGUIN BOOKS

PENGUIN BOOKS
Published by the Penguin Group
Penguin Putnam Inc., 375 Hudson Street,
New York, New York 10014, U.S.A.
Penguin Books Ltd, 27 Wrights Lane,
London W8 5TZ, England
Penguin Books Australia Ltd, Ringwood,
Victoria, Australia
Penguin Books Canada Ltd, 10 Alcorn Avenue,
Toronto, Ontario, Canada M4V 3B2
Penguin Books (N.Z.) Ltd, 182–190 Wairau Road,
Auckland 10, New Zealand
Penguin India, 210 Chiranjiv Tower, 43 Nehru Place,
New Delhi 11009, India

Penguin Books Ltd, Registered Offices:
Harmondsworth, Middlesex, England

First published in the United States of America by Viking Penguin,
a member of Penguin Putnam Inc. 1997
Published in Penguin Books 1998

1   3   5   7   9   10   8   6   4   2

Portions of this work first appeared in *Artes*, *Common Knowledge*
(published by Oxford University Press), *Granta*, and *West Coast Line*

THE LIBRARY OF CONGRESS HAS CATALOGUED THE HARDCOVER AS FOLLOWS:
Coetzee, J.M., date.
Boyhood: scenes from provincial life/J.M. Coetzee.
p.   cm.
ISBN 0-670-87220-2 (hc.)
ISBN 0 14 02.6566 X (pbk.)
1. Coetzee, J. M., date—Biography.   2. Authors, South African—20th century—
Biography.   I. Title.
PR9369.3.C58Z463   1997
823—dc21   97–12360
[B]

Printed in the United States of America
Set in Bodoni Book
Designed by Sabrina Bowers

BOYHOOD

Scenes from Provincial Life

ONE

THEY LIVE ON A HOUSING ESTATE outside the town of Worcester, between the railway line and the National Road. The streets of the estate have tree-names but no trees yet. Their address is No. 12 Poplar Avenue. All the houses on the estate are new and identical. They are set in large plots of red clay earth where nothing grows, separated by wire fences. In each back yard stands a small block consisting of a room and a lavatory. Though they have no servant, they refer to these as 'the servant's room' and 'the servant's lavatory.' They use the servant's room to store things in: newspapers, empty bottles, a broken chair, an old coir mattress.

At the bottom of the yard they put up a poultry-run and instal three hens, which are supposed to lay eggs for them. But the hens do not flourish. Rainwater, unable to seep away in the clay, stands in pools in the yard. The poultry run turns into an evil smelling morass. The hens develop gross swellings on their legs, like elephant-skin. Sickly and cross, they cease to lay. His mother consults her sister in Stellenbosch, who says they will return to laying only after the horny shells under their tongues have been cut out. So one after another his mother takes the hens between her knees, presses on their jowls till they open their beaks, and with the point of a paring-knife picks at their

1

tongues. The hens shriek and struggle, their eyes bulging. He shudders and turns away. He thinks of his mother slapping stewing-steak down on the kitchen counter and cutting it into cubes; he thinks of her bloody fingers.

The nearest shops are a mile away along a bleak eucalyptus-lined road. Trapped in this box of a house on the housing estate, there is nothing for his mother to do all day but sweep and tidy. Every time the wind blows, a fine ochre clay-dust whirls in under the doors, seeps through the cracks in the window-frames, under the eaves, through the joints of the ceiling. After a day-long storm the dust lies piled inches high against the front wall.

They buy a vacuum cleaner. Every morning his mother trails the vacuum cleaner from room to room, sucking up the dust into the roaring belly on which a smiling red goblin leaps as if over a hurdle. A goblin: why?

He plays with the vacuum cleaner, tearing up paper and watching the strips fly up the pipe like leaves in the wind. He holds the pipe over a trail of ants, sucking them up to their death.

There are ants in Worcester, flies, plagues of fleas. Worcester is only ninety miles from Cape Town, yet everything is worse here. He has a ring of fleabites above his socks, and scabs where he has scratched. Some nights he cannot sleep for the itching. He does not see why they ever had to leave Cape Town.

His mother is restless too. I wish I had a horse, she says. Then at least I could go riding in the veld. A horse! says his father: Do you want to be Lady Godiva?

She does not buy a horse. Instead, without warning, she buys a bicycle, a woman's model, second-hand, painted black. It is so huge and heavy that, when he experiments with it in the yard, he cannot turn the pedals.

She does not know how to ride a bicycle; perhaps she does not know how to ride a horse either. She bought the bicycle thinking that riding it would be a simple matter. Now she can find no one to teach her.

His father cannot hide his glee. Women do not ride bicycles, he says. His mother remains defiant. I will not be a prisoner in this house, she says. I will be free.

At first he had thought it splendid that his mother should have her own bicycle. He had even pictured the three of them riding together down Poplar Avenue, she and he and his brother. But now, as he listens to his father's jokes, which his mother can meet only with dogged silence, he begins to waver. Women don't ride bicycles: what if his father is right? If his mother can find no one willing to teach her, if no other housewife in Reunion Park has a bicycle, then perhaps women are indeed not supposed to ride bicycles.

Alone in the back yard, his mother tries to teach herself. Holding her legs out straight on either side, she rolls down the incline toward the chicken-run. The bicycle tips over and comes to a stop. Because it does not have a crossbar, she does not fall, merely staggers about in a silly way, clutching the handlebars.

His heart turns against her. That evening he joins in with his father's jeering. He is well aware what a betrayal this is. Now his mother is all alone.

Nevertheless she does learn to ride, though in an uncertain, wobbling way, straining to turn the heavy cranks.

She makes her expeditions to Worcester in the mornings, when he is at school. Only once does he catch a glimpse of her on her bicycle. She is wearing a white blouse and a dark skirt. She is coming down Poplar Avenue toward the house. Her hair streams in the wind. She looks young, like a girl, young and fresh and mysterious.

Every time his father sees the heavy black bicycle leaning

against the wall he makes jokes about it. In his jokes the citizens of Worcester interrupt their business to stand and gape as the woman on the bicycle labours past. *Trap! Trap!* they call out, mocking her: Push! There is nothing funny about the jokes, though he and his father always laugh together afterwards. As for his mother, she never has any repartee, she is not gifted in that way. 'Laugh if you like,' she says.

Then one day, without explanation, she stops riding the bicycle. Soon afterwards the bicycle disappears. No one says a word, but he knows she has been defeated, put in her place, and knows that he must bear part of the blame. I will make it up to her one day, he promises himself.

The memory of his mother on her bicycle does not leave him. She pedals away up Poplar Avenue, escaping from him, escaping towards her own desire. He does not want her to go. He does not want her to have a desire of her own. He wants her always to be in the house, waiting for him when he comes home. He does not often gang up with his father against her: his whole inclination is to gang up with her against his father. But in this case he belongs with the men.

TWO

HE SHARES NOTHING with his mother. His life at school is kept a tight secret from her. She shall know nothing, he resolves, but what appears on his quarterly report, which shall be impeccable. He will always come first in class. His conduct will always be Very Good, his progress Excellent. As long as the report is faultless, she will have no right to ask questions. That is the contract he establishes in his mind.

What happens at school is that boys are flogged. It happens every day. Boys are ordered to bend over and touch their toes and are flogged with a cane.

He has a classmate in Standard Three named Rob Hart whom the teacher particularly loves to beat. The Standard Three teacher is an excitable woman with hennaed hair named Miss Oosthuizen. From somewhere or other his parents know of her as Marie Oosthuizen: she takes part in theatricals and has never married. Clearly she has a life outside the school, but he cannot imagine it. He cannot imagine any teacher having a life outside school.

Miss Oosthuizen flies into rages, calls Rob Hart out from his desk, orders him to bend, and flogs him across the buttocks. The blows come fast one upon another, with barely time for the cane to swing back. By the time Miss Oosthuizen has finished with

5

him, Rob Hart is flushed in the face. But he does not cry; in fact, he may be flushed only because he was bending. Miss Oosthuizen, on the other hand, heaves at the breast and seems on the brink of tears—of tears and of other outpourings too.

After these spells of ungoverned passion the whole class is hushed, and remains hushed until the bell rings.

Miss Oosthuizen never succeeds in making Rob Hart cry; perhaps that is why she flies into such rages at him and beats him so hard, harder than anyone else. Rob Hart is the oldest boy in the class, nearly two years older than himself (he is the youngest); he has a sense that between Rob Hart and Miss Oosthuizen there is something going on that he is not privy to.

Rob Hart is tall and handsome in a devil-may-care way. Though Rob Hart is not clever and is perhaps even in danger of failing the standard, he is attracted toward him. Rob Hart is part of a world he has not yet found a way of entering: a world of sex and beating.

As for himself, he has no desire to be beaten by Miss Oosthuizen or anyone else. The very idea of being beaten makes him squirm with shame. There is nothing he will not do to save himself from it. In this respect he is unnatural and knows it. He comes from an unnatural and shameful family in which not only are children not beaten but older people are addressed by their first names and no one goes to church and shoes are worn every day.

Every teacher at his school, man or woman, has a cane and is at liberty to use it. Each of these canes has a personality, a character, which is known to the boys and talked about endlessly. In a spirit of knowing connoisseurship the boys weigh up the characters of the canes and the quality of pain they give, compare the arm and wrist techniques of the teachers who wield them. No one mentions the shame of being called out and made to bend and being beaten on one's backside.

Without experience of his own, he cannot take part in these conversations. Nevertheless, he knows that pain is not the most important consideration. If the other boys can bear the pain, then so can he, whose willpower is so much greater. What he will not be able to endure will be the shame. So bad will be the shame, he fears, so daunting, that he will hold tight to his desk and refuse to come when he is called out. And that will be a greater shame: it will set him apart, and set the other boys against him too. If it ever happens that he is called out to be beaten, there will be so humiliating a scene that he will never again be able to go back to school; in the end there will be no way out but to kill himself.

So that is what is at stake. That is why he never makes a sound in class. That is why he is always neat, why his homework is always done, why he always knows the answer. He dare not slip. If he slips, he risks being beaten; and whether he is beaten or whether he struggles against being beaten, it is all the same, he will die.

The strange thing is, it will only take one beating to break the spell of terror that has him in its grip. He is well aware of this: if, somehow, he can be rushed through the beating before he has had time to turn to stone and resist, if the violation of his body can be achieved quickly, by force, he will be able to come out on the other side a normal boy, able to join easily in discussion of the teachers and their canes and the various grades and flavours of pain they inflict. But by himself he cannot leap that barrier.

He puts the blame on his mother for not beating him. At the same time that he is glad he wears shoes and takes out books from the public library and stays away from school when he has a cold—all the things that set him apart—he is angry with his mother for not having normal children and making them live a normal life. His father, if his father were to take control, would turn them into a normal family. His father is normal in every way. He is grateful to his mother for protecting him from his father's normality, that is to say, from his father's occasional blue-eyed rages and threats to beat him. At the same time he is angry with his mother for turning him into something unnatural, something that needs to be protected if it is to continue to live.

Among the canes it is not Miss Oosthuizen's that leaves the deepest impression on him. The most fearsome cane is that of Mr Lategan the woodwork teacher. Mr Lategan's cane is not long and springy in the style most of the teachers prefer. Instead it is short and thick and stubby, more a stick or a baton than a switch. It is rumoured that Mr Lategan uses it only on the older boys, that it will be too much for a younger boy. It is rumoured that with his cane Mr Lategan has made even Matric boys blubber and plead for mercy and urinate in their pants and disgrace themselves.

Mr Lategan is a little man with close-cropped hair that stands upright, and a moustache. One of his thumbs is missing: the stub is neatly covered over with a purple scar. Mr Lategan hardly says anything. He is always in a distant, irritable mood, as though teaching woodwork to small boys is a task beneath him that he performs unwillingly. Through most of the lesson he stands at the window staring out over the quadrangle while the boys tentatively measure and saw and plane. Sometimes he has the stubby cane with him, idly tapping his trouser-leg while he ruminates. When he comes on his inspection round he disdainfully points to what is wrong, then with a shrug of the shoulders passes on.

It is permitted for boys to joke with teachers about their canes. In fact this is one area in which a certain teasing of the teachers is permitted. 'Make him sing, sir!' say the boys, and Mr Gouws will flash his wrist and his long cane (the longest cane in the school, though Mr Gouws is only the Standard Five teacher) will whistle through the air.

No one jokes with Mr Lategan. There is awe of Mr Lategan, of what he can do with his cane to boys who are almost men.

When his father and his father's brothers get together on the farm at Christmas, talk always turns to their schooldays. They reminisce about their schoolmasters and their schoolmasters' canes; they recall cold winter mornings when the cane would raise blue weals on their buttocks and the sting would linger for days in the memory of the flesh. In their words there is a note of nostalgia and pleasurable fear. He listens avidly but makes himself as inconspicuous as possible. He does not want them to turn to him, in some pause in the conversation, and ask about the place of the cane in his own life. He has never been beaten and is deeply ashamed of it. He cannot talk about canes in the easy, knowing way of these men.

He has a sense that he is damaged. He has a sense that something is slowly tearing inside him all the time: a wall, a membrane. He tried to hold himself as tight as possible to keep the tearing within bounds. To keep it within bounds, not to stop it: nothing will stop it.

Once a week he and his class troop across the school grounds to the gymnasium for PT, physical training. In the changing-room they put on white singlets and shorts. Then under the direction of Mr Barnard, also attired in white, they spend half an hour leapfrogging the pommel-horse or tossing the medicine ball or jumping and clapping their hands above their heads.

They do all of this with bare feet. For days ahead, he dreads baring his feet for PT, his feet that are always covered. Yet when his shoes and socks are off, it is suddenly not difficult at all. He has simply to remove himself from his shame, to go through with the undressing in a brisk, hurried way, and his feet become just feet like everyone else's. Somewhere in the vicinity the shame still hangs, waiting to return to him, but it is a private shame, which the other boys need never be aware of.

His feet are soft and white; otherwise they look like everyone else's, even those of boys who have no shoes and come to school barefoot. He does not enjoy PT and the stripping for PT, but he tells himself he can endure it, as he endures other things.

Then one day there is a change in the routine. They are sent from the gymnasium to the tennis courts to learn paddle tennis. The courts are some distance away; along the pathway he has to tread carefully, picking his steps among the pebbles. Under the summer sun the tarmac of the court itself is so hot that he has to hop from foot to foot to keep from burning. It is a relief to get back to the changing-room and put on his shoes again; but by afternoon he can barely walk, and when his mother removes his shoes at home she finds the soles of his feet blistered and bleeding.

He spends three days at home recovering. On the fourth day he returns with a note from his mother, a note whose indignant wording he is aware of and approves. Like a wounded warrior resuming his place in the ranks, he limps down the aisle to his desk.

'Why were you away from school?' whisper his classmates.

'I couldn't walk, I had blisters on my feet from the tennis,' he whispers back.

He expects astonishment and sympathy; instead he gets mirth. Even those of his classmates who wear shoes do not take his story seriously. Somehow they too have acquired hardened feet, feet that do not blister. He alone has soft feet, and soft feet, it is emerging, are no claim to distinction. All of a sudden he is isolated—he and, behind him, his mother.

THREE

HE HAS NEVER worked out the position of his father in the household. In fact, it is not obvious to him by what right his father is there at all. In a normal household, he is prepared to accept, the father stands at the head: the house belongs to him, the wife and children live under his sway. But in their own case, and in the households of his mother's two sisters as well, it is the mother and children who make up the core, while the husband is no more than an appendage, a contributor to the economy as a paying lodger might be.

As long as he can remember he has had a sense of himself as prince of the house, and of his mother as his dubious promoter and anxious protector—anxious, dubious because, he knows, a child is not meant to rule the roost. If there is anyone to be jealous of, it is not his father but his younger brother. For his mother promotes his brother too—promotes and even, because his brother is clever but not as clever as he, nor as bold or adventurous, favours him. In fact, his mother seems always to be hovering over his brother, ready to ward off danger; whereas in his own case she is only somewhere in the background, waiting, listening, ready to come if he should call.

He wants her to behave toward him as she does toward his

brother. But he wants this as a sign, a proof, no more. He knows that he will fly into a rage if she ever begins hovering over him.

He keeps driving her into corners, demanding that she admit whom she loves more, him or his brother. Always she slips the trap. 'I love you both the same,' she maintains, smiling. Even his most ingenious questions—what if the house were to catch fire, for instance, and she had time to rescue only one of them?—fail to snare her. 'Both of you,' she says, 'I will surely save both of you. But the house won't catch fire.' Though he mocks her for her literal-mindedness, he respects her dogged constancy.

His rages against his mother are one of the things he has to keep a careful secret from the world outside. Only the four of them know what torrents of scorn he pours upon her, how much like an inferior he treats her. 'If your teachers and your friends knew how you spoke to your mother . . . ,' says his father, wagging a finger meaningfully. He hates his father for seeing so clearly the chink in his armour.

He wants his father to beat him and turn him into a normal boy. At the same time he knows that if his father dared to strike him, he would not rest until he had his revenge. If his father were to hit him, he would go mad: he would become possessed, like a rat in a corner, hurtling about, snapping with its poisonous fangs, too dangerous to be touched.

At home he is an irascible despot, at school a lamb, meek and mild, who sits in the second row from the back, the most obscure row, so that he will not be noticed, and goes rigid with fear when the beating starts. By living this double life he has created for himself a burden of imposture. No one else has to bear anything like it, not even his brother, who is at most a nervous, wishy-washy imitation of himself. In fact, he suspects that at heart his brother may be normal. He is on his own. From no quarter can he expect support. It is up to him to somehow get beyond childhood, beyond family and school, to a new life where he will not need to pretend any more.

Childhood, says the *Children's Encyclopaedia*, is a time of innocent joy, to be spent in the meadows amid buttercups and bunny-rabbits or at the hearthside absorbed in a storybook. It is a vision of childhood utterly alien to him. Nothing he experiences in Worcester, at home or at school, leads him to think that childhood is anything but a time of gritting the teeth and enduring.

BECAUSE THERE IS NO Wolf Cub pack in Worcester, he is allowed to join the Boy Scout troop though he is only ten. For his inauguration as a Scout he prepares himself punctiliously. With his mother he goes to the outfitter's to buy the uniform: stiff olive-brown felt hat and silver hat-badge, khaki shirt and shorts and stockings, leather belt with Boy Scout clasp, green shoulder-tabs, green stocking-flashes. He cuts a five-foot stave from a poplar tree, peels off the bark, and spends an afternoon with a heated screwdriver burning into the white woodflesh the entire Morse and semaphore codes. He goes off to his first Scout meeting with this stave slung over his shoulder with a green cord that he has himself triple-braided. Taking the oath with a two-finger salute, he is by far the most impeccably outfitted of the new boys, the 'tenderfeet.'

Boy Scouts, he discovers, consists, like school, of passing examinations. For each examination you pass you get a badge, which you sew on to your shirt.

Examinations are taken in a preordained sequence. The first examination is in tying knots: the reef knot and the double reef, the sheepshank, the bowline. He passes it, but without distinction. It is not clear to him how one passes these Boy Scout examinations with distinction, how one excels.

The second examination is for a woodman's badge. To pass, he is required to light a fire, using no paper and striking no more than three matches. On the bare ground at the side of the Anglican church hall, on a winter's evening with a cold wind blowing, he assembles his heap of twigs and scraps of bark, and then, with his troop leader and the scoutmaster observing, strikes his matches one by one. Each time the fire does not take: each time the wind blows out the tiny flame. The scoutmaster and troop leader turn away. They do not utter the words, 'You have failed,' so he is not sure that he has in fact failed. What if they are going off to confer and decide that, because of the wind, the test was unfair? He waits for them to come back. He waits for the woodsman's badge to be given to him anyhow. But nothing happens. He stands by his pile of twigs and nothing happens.

No one ever mentions it again. It is the first examination he has failed in his life.

Every June vacation the Scout troop goes on a camp. Save for a week in hospital at the age of four he has never been away from his mother. But he is determined to go with the Scouts.

There is a list of things to take. One is a ground-sheet. His mother does not have a ground-sheet, is not even sure what a ground-sheet is. Instead she gives him an inflatable red rubber mattress. At the campsite he discovers that all the other boys have proper khaki-coloured ground-sheets. His red mattress at once sets him apart. Nor can he bring himself to move his bowels over a stinking pit in the earth.

On the third day of the camp they go swimming in the Breede River. Though, at the time when they lived in Cape Town, he and his brother and his cousin used to catch the train to Fish

Hoek and spend whole afternoons clambering on the rocks and making castles in the sand and splashing in the waves, he does not actually know how to swim. Now, as a Boy Scout, he must swim across the river and back.

He hates rivers for their murkiness, for the mud that oozes between his toes, for the rusty tin cans and broken bottles he could step on; he prefers clean white sea-sand. But he plunges in and somehow splashes across. On the far bank he clutches the root of a tree, finds a foothold, stands waist-deep in sullen brown water, his teeth chattering.

The other boys turn and begin to swim back. He is left alone. There is nothing to do but launch himself back into the water.

By midstream he is exhausted. He gives up swimming and tries to stand, but the river is too deep. His head goes under. He tries to lift himself, to swim again, but he has not the strength. He goes under a second time.

He has a vision of his mother sitting on a chair with a high, straight back reading the letter that tells of his death. His brother stands at her side, reading over her shoulder.

The next he knows, he is lying on the river-bank and his troop-leader, whose name is Michael but whom he has been too shy to speak to, is straddling him. He closes his eyes, filled with well-being. He has been saved.

For weeks afterwards he thinks of Michael, of how Michael risked his own life to plunge back into the river and rescue him. Each time it strikes him how wonderful it is that Michael should have noticed—noticed him, noticed that he was failing. Compared with Michael (who is in Standard Seven and has all except the most advanced badges and is going to be a King's Scout) he is negligible. It would have been quite appropriate for Michael not to have seen him go under, even not to have missed him until they got back to camp. Then all that would have been required of

Michael would have been to write the letter to his mother, the cool, formal letter beginning: 'We regret to inform you . . .'

From that day onward he knows there is something special about him. He should have died but he did not. Despite his unworthiness, he has been given a second life. He was dead but is alive.

Of what passed at the camp he breathes not a word to his mother.

FOUR

THE GREAT SECRET of his school life, the secret he tells no one at home, is that he has become a Roman Catholic, that for all practical purposes he 'is' a Roman Catholic.

The topic is difficult to raise at home because their family 'is' nothing. They are of course South Africans, but even South Africanness is faintly embarrassing, and therefore not talked about, since not everyone who lives in South Africa is a South African, or not a proper South African.

In religion they are certainly nothing. Not even in his father's family, which is much safer and more ordinary than his mother's, does anyone go to church. He himself has been in a church only twice in his life: once to be baptized and once to celebrate victory in World War Two.

The decision to 'be' a Roman Catholic is made on the spur of the moment. On the first morning at his new school, while the rest of the class is marched off to assembly in the school hall, he and the three other new boys are kept behind. 'What is your religion?' asks the teacher of each of them. He glances right and left. What is the right answer? What religions are there to choose from? Is it like Russians and Americans? His turn comes. 'What is your religion?' asks the teacher. He is sweating, he does not know what to say. 'Are you a Christian or a Roman

Catholic or a Jew?' she demands impatiently. 'Roman Catholic,' he says.

When the questioning is over, he and another boy who says he is a Jew are motioned to stay behind; the two who say they are Christians go off to assembly.

They wait to see what will happen to them. But nothing happens. The corridors are empty, the building is silent, there are no teachers left.

They wander into the playground, where they join the rag-tag of other boys left behind. It is marbles season; in the unfamiliar hush of the empty grounds, with dove-calls in the air and the faint, far-off sound of singing, they play marbles. Time passes. Then the bell rings for the end of assembly. The rest of the boys return from the hall, marching in files, class by class. Some appear to be in a bad mood. *'Jood!'* an Afrikaans boy hisses at him as he passes: Jew! When they rejoin their class, no one smiles.

The episode disturbs him. He hopes that the next day he and the other new boys will be kept behind again and asked to make new choices. Then he, who has clearly made a mistake, can correct himself and be a Christian. But there is no second chance.

Twice a week the separation of sheep from goats is repeated. While Jews and Catholics are left to their own devices, the Christians go off to assembly to sing hymns and be preached to. In revenge for which, and in revenge for what the Jews did to Christ, the Afrikaans boys, big, brutal, knobbly, sometimes catch a Jew or a Catholic and punch him in the biceps, short, vicious knuckle-punches, or knee him in the balls, or twist his arms behind his back till he pleads for mercy. *'Asseblief!'* the boy whimpers: Please! *'Jood!'* they hiss back: *'Jood! Vuilgoed!'* Jew! Filth!

One day during the lunch break two Afrikaans boys corner him and drag him to the farthest corner of the rugby field. One of them is huge and fat. He pleads with them. '*Ek is nie 'n Jood nie,*' he says: I am not a Jew. He offers to let them ride his bicycle, offers them his bicycle for the afternoon. The more he gabbles, the more the fat boy smiles. This is evidently what he likes: the pleading, the abasement.

From his shirt pocket the fat boy produces something, something that begins to explain why he has been dragged to this quiet corner: a wriggling green caterpillar. The friend pins his arms behind his back; the fat boy pinches the hinges of his jaws till his mouth opens, then forces the caterpillar in. He spits it out, already torn, already exuding its juices. The fat boy crushes it, smears it over his lips. '*Jood!*' he says, wiping his hand clean on the grass.

He chose to be a Roman Catholic, that fateful morning, because of Rome, because of Horatius and his two comrades, swords in their hands, crested helmets on their heads, indomitable courage in their glance, defending the bridge over the Tiber against the Etruscan hordes. Now, step by step, he discovers from the other Catholic boys what a Roman Catholic really is. A Roman Catholic has nothing to do with Rome. Roman Catholics have not even heard of Horatius. Roman Catholics go to catechism on Friday afternoons; they go to confession; they take communion. That is what Roman Catholics do.

The older Catholic boys corner him and quiz him: has he been to catechism, has he been to confession, has he taken communion? Catechism? Confession? Communion? He does not even know what the words mean. 'I used to go in Cape Town,' he says evasively. 'Where?' they say. He does not know the names of any churches in Cape Town, but nor do they. 'Come to catechism on Friday,' they order him. When he does not come, they inform the priest that there is an apostate in Standard Three. The priest sends a message, which they relay: he must come to catechism. He suspects they have fabricated the message, but the next Friday he stays at home, lying low.

The older Catholic boys begin to make it clear they do not believe his stories about being a Catholic in Cape Town. But he has gone too far now, there is no going back. If he says, 'I made a mistake, I am actually a Christian,' he will be disgraced. Besides, even if he has to bear the taunts of the Afrikaners and the interrogations of the real Catholics, are the two free periods a week not worth it, free periods to walk around the empty playing-fields talking to the Jews?

One Saturday afternoon when the whole of Worcester, stunned by the heat, has gone to sleep, he takes out his bicycle and cycles to Dorp Street.

Usually he gives Dorp Street a wide berth, since that is where the Catholic church is. But today the street is empty, there is no sound but the rustle of water in the furrows. Nonchalantly he cycles past, pretending not to look.

The church is not as big as he thought it would be. It is a low, blank building with a little statue over the portico: the Virgin, hooded, holding her baby.

He reaches the bottom of the street. He would like to turn and come back for a second look, but he is afraid of stretching his luck, afraid that a priest in black will emerge and wave for him to stop.

The Catholic boys nag him and make sneering remarks, the Christians persecute him, but the Jews do not judge. The Jews pretend not to notice. The Jews wear shoes too. In a minor way he feels comfortable with the Jews. The Jews are not so bad.

Nevertheless, with Jews one has to tread carefully. For the Jews are everywhere, the Jews are taking over the country. He hears this on all sides, but particularly from his uncles, his mother's two bachelor brothers, when they visit. Norman and

Lance come every summer, like migrating birds, though rarely at the same time. They sleep on the sofa, get up at eleven in the morning, moon around the house for hours, half-dressed, tousled. Both have cars; sometimes they can be persuaded to take one for an afternoon drive, but they seem to prefer passing their time smoking and drinking tea and talking about the old days. Then they have supper, and after supper, play poker or rummy until midnight with whoever can be persuaded to stay up.

He loves to listen to his mother and his uncles going for the thousandth time over the events of their childhood on the farm. He is never happier than when listening to these stories, to the teasing and the laughter that go with them. His friends do not come from families with stories like these. That is what sets him apart: the two farms behind him, his mother's farm, his father's farm, and the stories of those farms. Through the farms he is rooted in the past; through the farms he has substance.

There is a third farm too: Skipperskloof, near Williston. His family has no roots there, it is a farm they have married into. Nevertheless, Skipperskloof is important too. All farms are important. Farms are places of freedom, of life.

In among the stories that Norman and Lance and his mother tell flit the figures of Jews, comic, sly, but also cunning and heartless, like jackals. Jews from Oudtshoorn came to the farm every year to buy ostrich feathers from their father, his grandfather. They persuaded him to give up wool and farm only with ostriches. Ostriches would make him rich, they said. Then one day the bottom fell out of the ostrich-feather market. The Jews refused to buy any more feathers and his grandfather went bankrupt. Everyone in the district went bankrupt and the Jews took over their farms. That is how the Jews operate, says Norman: you must never trust a Jew.

His father demurs. His father cannot afford to decry the Jews, since he is employed by a Jew. Standard Canners, where he works as a bookkeeper, belongs to Wolf Heller. In fact it was Wolf Heller who brought him from Cape Town to Worcester when he lost his job in the civil service. The future of their family is bound up with the future of Standard Canners, which, in the few years since he took it over, Wolf Heller has built up into a giant of the canning world. There are wonderful prospects in Standard Canners, says his father, for someone like himself, with legal qualifications.

So Wolf Heller is exempted from the general strictures on Jews. Wolf Heller takes care of his employees. At Christmas he even gives them presents, though Christmas means nothing to Jews.

There are no Heller children at school in Worcester. If there are Heller children at all, they have presumably been sent to SACS in Cape Town, which is a Jewish school in all but name. Nor are there Jewish families in Reunion Park. The Jews of Worcester live in the older, greener, shadier part of the town. Though there are Jewish boys in his class, he is never invited into their homes. He sees them only at school, brought closer to them during assembly periods, when Jews and Catholics are isolated and subjected to the ire of the Christians.

Every now and again, however, for reasons that are not clear, the dispensation that allows them freedom during assembly is withdrawn and they are summoned to the hall.

The hall is always packed. Senior boys occupy the seats, while boys from the junior school crowd the floor. The Jews and Catholics—perhaps twenty in all—thread their way among them, looking for space. Hands surreptitiously snatch at their ankles, trying to trip them.

The *dominee* is already on the stage, a pale young man in a black suit and white tie. He preaches in a high, sing-song voice, drawing out the long vowels, pronouncing every letter of every word punctiliously. When the preaching is over, they have to stand for the prayer. What is it proper for a Catholic to do during a Christian prayer? Does he close his eyes and move his lips, or does he pretend not to be there? He cannot see any of the real Catholics; he puts on a blank look and allows his eyes to go out of focus.

The *dominee* sits down. The songbooks are handed out; it is time for the singing. One of the women teachers steps forward to conduct. *'Al die veld is vrolik, al die voëltjies sing,'* sing the juniors. Then the seniors stand up. *'Uit die blou van onse hemel,'* they sing in their deep voices, standing to attention, gazing sternly ahead: the national anthem, *their* national anthem. Tentatively, nervously, the younger boys join in. Leaning over them, waving with her arms as though scooping feathers, the teacher tries to uplift them, encourage them. *'Ons sal antwoord op jou roepstem, ons sal offer wat jy vra,'* they sing: we will answer your call.

At last it is over. The teachers descend from the platform, first the principal, then the *dominee*, then the rest of them. The boys file out of the hall. A fist strikes him in the kidneys, a short, quick jab, invisible. *'Jood!'* a voice whispers. Then he is out, he is free, he can breathe fresh air again.

Despite the menaces of the real Catholics, despite the hovering possibility that the priest will visit his parents and unmask him, he is thankful for the inspiration that made him choose Rome. He is grateful to the Church that shelters him; he has no regrets, does not wish to stop being a Catholic. If being a Christian means singing hymns and listening to sermons and then coming out to torment the Jews, he has no wish to be a Christian. The fault is not his if the Catholics of Worcester are Catholic without being Roman, if they know nothing about Horatius and his comrades holding the bridge over the Tiber ('Tiber, Father Tiber, to whom we Romans pray'), about Leonidas and his Spartans holding the pass at Thermopylae, about Roland holding the pass against the Saracens. He can think of nothing more heroic than holding a pass, nothing nobler than giving up one's life to save other people, who will afterwards weep over one's corpse. That is what he would like to be: a hero. That is what proper Roman Catholicism should be about.

It is a summer evening, cool after the long, hot day. He is in the public gardens, where he has been playing cricket with Greenberg and Goldstein: Greenberg, who is solid in class but not good at cricket; Goldstein, who has large brown eyes and wears sandals and is quite dashing. It is late, well past seven-thirty. Save for the three of them, the gardens are deserted. They have had to give up their cricket: it is too dark to see the ball. So they have wrestling fights as if they were children again, rolling about on the grass, tickling each other, laughing and giggling. He stands up, takes a deep breath. A surge of exultation passes through him. He thinks, 'I have never been happier in my life. I would like to be with Greenberg and Goldstein forever.'

They part. It is true. He would like to live like this forever, riding his bicycle through the wide and empty streets of Worcester in the dusk of a summer's day, when all the other children have been called in and he alone is abroad, like a king.

FIVE

BEING A CATHOLIC is a part of his life reserved for school. Prefer-
ring the Russians to the Americans is a secret so dark that he
can reveal it to no one. Liking the Russians is a serious matter.
It can have you ostracized.

In a box in his cupboard he keeps the book of drawings he did
at the height of his passion for the Russians in 1947. The drawings, in heavy lead pencil coloured in with wax crayons, show
Russian planes shooting American planes out of the sky, Russian ships sinking American ships. Though the fervour of that
year, when a wave of enmity against the Russians suddenly
burst out on the radio and everyone had to take sides, has sub-
sided, he retains his secret loyalty: loyalty to the Russians,
but even more loyalty to himself as he was when he did the
drawings.

There is no one here in Worcester who knows he likes the
Russians. In Cape Town there used to be his friend Nicky, with
whom he played war games with lead soldiers and a spring-
loaded cannon that fired matchsticks; but when he found how
dangerous his allegiances were, what he stood to lose, he first
swore Nicky to secrecy, then, to make doubly sure, told him he
had changed sides and liked the Americans.

26

In Worcester no one but he likes the Russians. His loyalty to the Red Star sets him absolutely apart.

Where did he pick up this infatuation, that strikes even him as odd? His mother's name is Vera: Vera, with its icy capital *V*, an arrow plunging downwards. Vera, she once told him, was a Russian name. When the Russians and the Americans were first set before him as antagonists between whom he had to choose ('Who do you like, Smuts or Malan? Who do you like, Superman or Captain Marvel? Who do you like, the Russians or the Americans?'), he chose the Russians as he chose the Romans: because he likes the letter *r*, particularly the capital *R*, the strongest of all the letters.

He chose the Russians in 1947 when everyone else was choosing the Americans; having chosen them, he threw himself into reading about them. His father had bought a three-volume history of World War Two. He loved these books and pored over them, pored over photographs of Russian soldiers in white ski uniforms, Russian soldiers with tommy-guns dodging among the ruins of Stalingrad, Russian tank commanders staring ahead through their binoculars. (The Russian T-34 was the best tank in the world, better than the American Sherman, better even than the German Tiger.) Again and again he came back to a painting of a Russian pilot banking his dive-bomber over a burning and devastated German tank column. He adopted everything Russian. He adopted stern but fatherly Field-Marshal Stalin, the greatest and most far-sighted strategist of the war; he adopted the borzoi, the Russian wolfhound, swiftest of all dogs. He knew everything there was to know about Russia: its land area in square miles, its coal and steel output in tons, the length of each of its great rivers, the Volga, the Dnieper, the Yenisei, the Ob.

Then came the realization, from the disapproval of his parents, from the puzzlement of his friends, from what they reported when they told their own parents about him: liking the Russians was not part of a game, it was not allowed.

Always, it seems, there is something that goes wrong. Whatever he wants, whatever he likes, has sooner or later to be turned into a secret. He begins to think of himself as one of those spiders that live in a hole in the ground with a trapdoor. Always the spider has to be scuttling back into its hole, closing the trapdoor behind it, shutting out the world, hiding.

In Worcester he keeps his Russian past a secret, hides the reprehensible book of drawings, with their smoke-trails of enemy fighters crashing into the ocean and battleships sliding bow-first under the waves. For drawing he substitutes games of imaginary cricket. He uses a wooden beach-bat and a tennis ball. The challenge is to keep the ball in the air as long as possible. For hours on end he circles the dining-room table patting the ball in the air. All the vases and ornaments have been cleared away; every time the ball strikes the ceiling a shower of fine red dust descends.

He plays entire games, eleven batsmen a side each batting twice. Each hit counts as a run. When his attention flags and he misses the ball a batsman is out, and he enters his score on the scorecard. Huge totals mount up: five hundred runs, six hundred runs. Once England scores a thousand runs, which no real team has ever done before. Sometimes England wins, sometimes South Africa; more rarely Australia or New Zealand.

Russia and America do not play cricket. The Americans play baseball; the Russians do not appear to play anything, perhaps because it is always snowing there.

He does not know what the Russians do when they are not making war.

Of his private cricket games he says nothing to his friends, keeping them for home. Once, during their early months in Worcester, a boy from his class had wandered in through the open front door and found him lying on his back under a chair. 'What are you doing there?' he had asked. 'Thinking,' he had replied unthinkingly: 'I like thinking.' Soon everyone in his class knew about it: the new boy was odd, he wasn't normal. From that mistake he has learned to be more prudent. Part of being prudent is always to tell less rather than more.

He also plays proper cricket with whoever is prepared to play. But proper cricket on the empty square in the middle of Reunion Park is too slow to be borne: the ball is forever being missed by the batsman, missed by the wicketkeeper, getting lost. He hates searching for lost balls. He hates fielding too, on stony ground where you bloody your hands and knees every time you fall. He wants to bat or bowl, that is all.

He courts his brother, though his brother is only six years old, promising to let him play with his toys if he will bowl to him in the back yard. His brother bowls for a while, then grows bored and sullen and scuttles indoors for protection. He tries to teach his mother to bowl, but she cannot master the action. While he grows exasperated, she quivers with laughter at her own clumsiness. So he allows her to throw the ball instead. But in the end the spectacle is too shameful, too easily seen from the street: a mother playing cricket with her son.

He cuts a jam-tin in half and nails the bottom half to a two-foot wooden arm. He mounts the arm on an axle through the walls of a packing-case weighed down with bricks. The arm is drawn forward by a strip of inner-tube rubber, drawn back by a rope that runs through a hook on the packing-case. He puts a ball in the tin cup, retreats ten yards, pulls on the rope till the rubber is taut, anchors the rope under his heel, takes up his batting position, and releases the rope. Sometimes the ball shoots up into the sky, sometimes straight at his head; but every now and again it flies within reach and he is able to hit it. With this he is satisfied: he has bowled and batted all by himself, he has triumphed, nothing is impossible.

One day, in a mood of reckless intimacy, he asks Greenberg and Goldstein to bring out their earliest memories. Greenberg demurs: it is a game he is not willing to play. Goldstein tells a long and pointless story about being taken to the beach, a story he barely listens to. For the point of the game is, of course, to allow him to recount his own first memory.

He is leaning out of the window of their flat in Johannesburg. Dusk is falling. Out of the distance a car comes racing down the street. A dog, a small spotted dog, runs in front of it. The car hits the dog: its wheels go right over the dog's middle. With its hind legs paralysed, the dog drags itself away, squealing with pain. No doubt it will die; but at this point he is snatched away from the window.

It is a magnificent first memory, trumping anything that poor Goldstein can dredge up. But is it true? Why was he leaning out of the window watching an empty street? Did he really see the car hit the dog, or did he just hear a dog howling, and run to the window? Is it possible that he saw nothing but a dog dragging its hindquarters and made up the car and the driver and the rest of the story?

There is another first memory, one that he trusts more fully but would never repeat, certainly not to Greenberg and Goldstein, who would trumpet it around the school and turn him into a laughing-stock.

He is sitting beside his mother in a bus. It must be cold, for he is wearing red woollen leggings and a woollen cap with a bobble. The engine of the bus labours; they are ascending the wild and desolate Swartberg Pass.

In his hand is a sweet-wrapper. He holds the wrapper out of the window, which is open a crack. It flaps and trembles in the wind.

'Shall I let go?' he asks his mother.

She nods. He lets it go.

The scrap of paper flies up into the sky. Below there is nothing but the grim abyss of the pass, ringed with cold mountain-peaks. Craning backwards, he catches a last glimpse of the paper, still bravely flying.

'What will happen to it?' he asks his mother; but she does not comprehend.

That is the other first memory, the secret one. He thinks all the time of the scrap of paper, alone in all that vastness, that he abandoned when he should not have abandoned it. One day he must go back to the Swartberg Pass and find it and rescue it. That is his duty: he may not die until he has done it.

HIS MOTHER IS FULL OF SCORN for men who are 'useless with their hands,' among whom she numbers his father, but also her own brothers, and principally her eldest brother Roland, who could have kept the farm if he had worked hard enough to pay off its debts, but did not. Of the many uncles on his father's side (he counts eight by blood, another eight by marriage), the one she admires most is Joubert Olivier, who on Skipperskloof has installed an electric generator and has even taught himself dentistry. (On one of his visits to the farm he gets a toothache. Uncle Joubert seats him on a chair under a tree and, without anaesthetic, drills out the hole and fills it with gutta-percha. He has never suffered such agony in his life.)

When things break—plates, ornaments, toys—his mother fixes them herself: with string, with glue. The things she ties together come loose, since she does not know about knots. The things she glues together fall apart; she blames the glue.

The kitchen drawers are full of bent nails, lengths of string, balls of tinfoil, old stamps. 'Why are we saving them?' he asks. 'In case,' she replies.

In her angrier moods she denounces all book-learning. Children should be sent to trade school, she says, then put to work. Studying is just nonsense. Learning to be a cabinet-maker or a carpenter, learning to work with wood, is best. She is disenchanted with farming: now that farmers have suddenly become wealthy there is too much idleness among them, too much ostentation.

For the price of wool is rocketing. According to the radio, the Japanese are paying a pound a pound for the best grades. Sheep-farmers are buying new cars and taking seaside holidays. 'You must give us some of your money, now that you are so rich,' she tells Uncle Son on one of their visits to Voëlfontein. She smiles as she speaks, pretending it is a joke, but it is not funny. Uncle Son looks embarrassed, murmurs a reply he does not catch.

The farm was not meant to go to Uncle Son alone, his mother tells him: it was bequeathed to all twelve sons and daughters in equal portions. To save it from being auctioned, the sons and daughters agreed to sell their portions to Son; from that sale they came away with IOUs for a few pounds each. Now, because of the Japanese, the farm is worth thousands of pounds. Son ought to share his money.

He is ashamed of his mother for the crudeness with which she talks about money.

'You must become a doctor or an attorney,' she tells him. 'Those are the people who make money.' However, at other times she tells him that attorneys are all crooks. He does not ask how his father fits into this picture, his father the attorney who did not make money.

Doctors are not interested in their patients, she says. They just give you pills. Afrikaans doctors are the worst, because they are incompetent as well.

She says so many different things at different times that he does not know what she really thinks. He and his brother argue with her, point out the contradictions. If she thinks farmers are better than attorneys, why did she marry an attorney? If she thinks book-learning is nonsense, why did she become a teacher? The more they argue with her the more she smiles. She takes so much pleasure in her children's skill with words that she concedes every point, barely defending herself, willing them to win.

He does not share her pleasure. He does not think these arguments funny. He wishes she would believe in something. Her sweeping judgments, born out of passing moods, exasperate him.

As for him, he will probably become a teacher. That will be his life when he grows up. It seems a dull kind of life, but what else is there? For a long time he was going to become an engine-driver. 'What are you going to be when you grow up?' his aunts and uncles used to ask. 'An engine-driver!' he would pipe up, and everyone would nod and smile. Now he understands that 'Engine-driver' is what all small boys are expected to say, just as small girls are expected to say 'Nurse.' He is no longer small now, he belongs to the big world; he will have to put aside the fantasy of driving a great iron horse and do the realistic thing. He is good at school, there is nothing else he knows of that he is good at, therefore he will stay on at school, moving up through the ranks. One day, perhaps, he will even become an inspector. Anyhow, he will not take an office job: he cannot face working from morning to night with only two weeks' holiday a year.

What sort of teacher will he make? He can picture himself only dimly. He sees a figure in sports jacket and grey flannels (that is what men teachers seem to wear) walking down a corridor with books under its arm. It is only a glimpse, and in a moment it vanishes. He does not see the face.

He hopes that, when the day comes, he will not be sent to teach in a place like Worcester. But perhaps Worcester is a purgatory one must pass through. Perhaps Worcester is where people are sent to be tested.

One day they are given an essay to write in class: 'What I do in the mornings.' They are supposed to write about the things they do before setting off for school. He knows what is expected: how he makes his bed, how he washes the breakfast dishes, how he cuts his sandwiches for lunch. Though in fact he does none of these things—his mother does them for him—he lies well enough not to be found out. But he goes too far when he describes how he brushes his shoes. He has never brushed his own shoes in his life. In his essay he says you use the brush to brush the dirt off, after which you coat the shoe with polish. Miss Oosthuizen puts a big blue exclamation mark in the margin next to the shoe-brushing. He is mortified, prays that she will not call him out in front of the class to read his essay. That evening he watches carefully as his mother brushes his shoes, so that he will not get it wrong again.

He lets his mother brush his shoes as he lets her do everything for him that she wants to. The only thing that he will not let her do any more is to come into the bathroom when he is naked.

He knows he is a liar, knows he is bad, but he does not change. He does not change because he does not want to change. His difference from other boys may be bound up with his mother and his unnatural family, but is bound up with his lying too. If he stopped lying he would have to polish his shoes and talk politely and do everything that normal boys do. In that case he would no longer be himself. If he were no longer himself, what point would there be in living?

He is a liar and he is cold-hearted too: a liar to the world in general, cold-hearted toward his mother. It pains his mother, he can see, that he is steadily growing away from her. Nevertheless he hardens his heart and will not relent. His only excuse is that he is merciless to himself too. He lies but he does not lie to himself.

'When are you going to die?' he asks her one day, challenging her, surprised at his own daring.

'I am not going to die,' she replies. She speaks gaily, but there is something false in her gaiety.

'What if you get cancer?'

'You only get cancer if you are hit on the breast. I won't get cancer. I'll live forever. I won't die.'

He knows why she is saying this. She is saying it for him and his brother, so that they will not worry. It is a silly thing to say, but he is grateful to her for it.

He cannot imagine her dying. She is the firmest thing in his life. She is the rock on which he stands. Without her he would be nothing.

She guards her breasts carefully in case they are knocked. His very first memory, earlier than the dog, earlier than the scrap of paper, is of her white breasts. He suspects he must have hurt them when he was a baby, beaten them with his fists, otherwise she would not now deny them to him so pointedly, she who denies him nothing else.

Cancer is the great fear of her life. As for him, he has been taught to be wary of pains in his side, to treat each twinge as a sign of appendicitis. Will the ambulance get him to hospital before his appendix bursts? Will he ever wake up from the anaesthetic? He does not like to think of being cut open by a strange doctor. On the other hand, it would be nice to have a scar afterwards to show people. When peanuts and raisins are doled out during break at school, he blows away the papery red skins of the peanuts, which are reputed to collect in the appendix and fester there.

He absorbs himself in his collections. He collects stamps. He collects lead soldiers. He collects cards—cards of Australian cricketers, cards of English footballers, cards of cars of the world. To get the cards he has to buy packets of cigarettes made of nougat and icing-sugar, with pink-painted tips. His pockets are forever full of wilting, sticky cigarettes that he has forgotten to eat.

He spends hours on end with his Meccano set, showing his mother that he too can be good with his hands. He builds a windmill with sets of coupled pulleys whose blades can be cranked so fast that a breeze wafts across the room.

He trots around the yard tossing a cricket ball in the air and catching it without breaking his stride. What is the true trajectory of the ball: is it going straight up and straight down, as he sees it, or is it rising and falling in loops, as a motionless bystander would see it? When he talks to his mother about things like this, he sees the desperation in her eyes: she knows these things are important, and wants to understand why, but cannot. For his part, he wishes she would be interested in things for their own sake, not just because they interest him.

When there is something practical to be done that he cannot do and she cannot do, like fixing a leaking tap, she calls in a

Coloured man off the street, any man, any passer-by. Why, he asks in exasperation, does she have this faith in Coloured people? Because they are used to working with their hands, she replies. *Because* they have not gone to school, *because* they have no book-learning, she seems to be saying, they know how things in the real world work.

It is a silly thing to believe, particularly when these strangers reveal that they have no idea of how to fix a tap or repair a stove. Yet it is so different from what everyone else believes, so eccentric, that despite himself he finds it endearing. He would rather that his mother expected wonders of Coloured people than expected nothing of them at all.

He is always trying to make sense of his mother. Jews are exploiters, she says; yet she prefers Jewish doctors because they know what they are doing. Coloured people are the salt of the earth, she says, yet she and her sisters are always gossiping about pretend-whites with secret Coloured backgrounds. He cannot understand how she can hold so many contradictory beliefs at the same time. Yet at least she has beliefs. Her brothers too. Her brother Norman believes in the monk Nostradamus and his prophecies of the end of the world; he believes in flying saucers that land during the night and take people away. He cannot imagine his father or his father's family talking about the end of the world. Their one goal in life is to avoid controversy, to offend no one, to be amiable all the time; by comparison with his mother's family they are bland and boring.

He is too close to his mother, his mother is too close to him. That is the reason why, despite the hunting and all the other manly things he does during his visits to the farm, his father's family has never taken him to its bosom. His grandmother may have been too harsh in denying the three of them a home when, in 1944, they were living on half a lance-corporal's pay, too poor to buy butter or tea, but her instinct was right. The family, led by his grandmother, is not blind to the secret of No. 12 Poplar Avenue, which is that the eldest child is first in the household, the second child second, and the man, the husband, the father, last. Either his mother does not care enough to conceal it from the family or else his father has been complaining in private. In this perversion of the natural order they find something deeply insulting to their son and brother and therefore to themselves. They disapprove and, without being rude, do not hide their disapproval.

Sometimes, when she is quarrelling with his father and wants to score a point, his mother complains bitterly about being treated coldly by his family. Mostly, however—for her son's sake, because she knows how central the farm is to his life, because she can offer nothing to take its place—she tries to ingratiate herself with them in ways he finds distasteful. These efforts of hers go along with her jokes about money that are not jokes. She has no pride. Or to put it another way: she will do anything for him.

He wishes she would be normal. If she were normal, he could be normal.

It is the same with her two sisters. They have one child each, one son, over whom they hover with suffocating solicitude. His cousin Juan in Johannesburg is his closest friend in the world: they write letters to each other, they look forward to holidays together at the sea. Nevertheless, he does not like to see Juan shamefacedly obeying his mother's every instruction, even when she is not there to check. Of all the four sons, he is the only one who is not wholly under his mother's thumb. He has broken away, or half broken away: he has his own friends, whom he has chosen for himself, he goes out on his bicycle without saying where he is going or when he will be back. His cousins and his brother have no friends. He thinks of them as pale, timid, always at home under the eye of their fierce mothers. His father calls the three sister-mothers the three witches. 'Double, double, toil and trouble,' he says, quoting *Macbeth*. Delightedly, maliciously he agrees.

When his mother feels particularly bitter about her life in Reunion Park, she says she wishes she had married Bob Breech. He does not take her seriously. At the same time he cannot believe his ears. If she had married Bob Breech, where would he have been? Who would he have been? Would he have been Bob Breech's child? Would Bob Breech's child have been him?

Only one piece of evidence remains of a real Bob Breech. He comes across it by accident in one of his mother's albums: a blurred photograph of two young men in long white trousers and dark blazers standing on a beach with their arms around each other's shoulders, squinting into the sun. One of them he knows: Juan's father. Who is this other man? he asks his mother idly. Bob Breech, she replies. Where is he now? He is dead, she says.

He stares hard into the face of the dead Bob Breech. He can find nothing of himself there.

He does not inquire further. But, listening to the sisters, putting two and two together, he learns that Bob Breech came to South Africa for his health; that after a year or two he went back to England; that there he died. He died of consumption, but a broken heart, it is implied, may have contributed to his end, a broken heart because of the dark-haired, dark-eyed, wary-looking young schoolteacher whom he met at Plettenberg Bay and who would not marry him.

He loves to page through the albums. No matter how indistinct the photograph, he can always pick his mother out from the group: the one in whose shy, defensive look he recognizes a feminine version of his own. In the albums he follows her life through the 1920s and 1930s: first the team pictures (hockey, tennis), then the pictures from her tour of Europe: Scotland, Norway, Switzerland, Germany; Edinburgh, the fjords, the Alps, Bingen on the Rhine. Among her mementoes there is a propelling pencil from Bingen, with a tiny peephole in its side allowing a view of a castle perched on a cliff.

Sometimes they page through the albums together, he and she. She sighs and says she wishes she could see Scotland again, the heather, the bluebells. He thinks: she had a life before I was born. He is glad for her sake, since she has no life any more.

Her Europe is quite another Europe from the Europe of his father's photograph album, in which South Africans in khaki uniform strike poses against the pyramids of Egypt or against the rubble of Italian cities. But in this album he spends less time on the photographs than on the pamphlets interspersed with them, pamphlets dropped on the Allied positions from German aeroplanes. One tells the soldiers how to give themselves a temperature (by eating soap); another pictures a glamorous woman perched on the knee of a fat Jew with a hooked nose, drinking champagne. 'Do you know where your wife is tonight?' asks the subtitle. And then there is the blue porcelain eagle that his father found in the ruins of a house in Naples and brought back in his kit-bag, the eagle of empire that now stands on the desk in the living-room.

He is immensely proud of his father's war service. He is surprised—and gratified—to find how few of the fathers of his friends fought in the war. Why his father only became a lance-corporal he is not sure: he quietly leaves out the *lance-* when he repeats his father's adventures to his friends. But he treasures the photograph, taken in a studio in Cairo, of his handsome father sighting down a rifle barrel, one eye closed, his hair neatly combed, his beret tucked in regulation fashion under his epaulette. If he had his way it would be on the mantelshelf too.

His father and his mother differ about the Germans. His father likes the Italians (their heart was not in the fight, he says: all they wanted to do was surrender and go back home) but hates the Germans. He tells the story of a German shot while he was sitting on the privy. Sometimes, in the story, it was he who shot the German, sometimes one of his friends; but in none of the versions does he show any pity, only amusement at the German's confusion as he tried to raise his hands and pull up his pants at the same time.

His mother knows it is not a good idea to praise the Germans too openly, but sometimes, when he and his father gang up on her, will leave discretion behind. 'The Germans are the best people in the world,' she will say. 'It was that terrible Hitler who led them into so much suffering.'

Her brother Norman disagrees. 'Hitler gave the Germans pride in themselves,' he says.

His mother and Norman travelled through Europe together in the 1930s: not only through Norway and the highlands of Scotland but through Germany, Hitler's Germany. Their family—the Brechers, the du Biels—is from Germany, or at least from Pomerania, which is now in Poland. Is it good to be from Pomerania? He is not sure. But at least he knows where he comes from.

'The Germans didn't want to fight against the South Africans,' says Norman. 'They like the South Africans. If it hadn't been for Smuts we would never have gone to war against Germany. Smuts was a *skelm*, a crook. He sold us to the British.'

His father and Norman do not like each other. When his father wants to get at his mother, in their late-night quarrels in the kitchen, he taunts her about her brother who did not join up, but marched with the Ossewabrandwag instead. 'That's a lie!' she maintains angrily. 'Norman was not in the Ossewabrandwag. Ask him yourself, he will tell you.'

When he asks his mother what the Ossewabrandwag is, she says it is just nonsense, people who marched in the streets with torches.

The fingers of Norman's right hand are yellow with nicotine. He lives in a hotel room in Pretoria and has lived there for years. He makes his money by selling a pamphlet he has written about ju-jitsu, which he advertises in the classified pages of the *Pretoria News*. 'Learn the Japanese art of self-defence,' says the advertisement. 'Six easy lessons.' People send him ten-shilling postal orders and he sends them the pamphlet: a single page folded in four, with sketches of the various holds. When ju-jitsu does not bring in enough money, he sells plots on commission for an estate agency. He stays in bed till noon every day, drinking tea and smoking and reading stories in *Argosy* and *Lilliput*. In the afternoons he plays tennis. In 1938, twelve years ago, he was the Western Province singles champion. He still has ambitions of playing at Wimbledon, in the doubles, if he can find a partner.

At the end of his visit, before he leaves for Pretoria, Norman takes him aside and slips a brown ten-shilling note into his shirt pocket. 'For ice-cream,' he murmurs: the same words every year. He likes Norman not only for the present—ten shillings is a lot of money—but for remembering, for never failing to remember.

His father prefers the other brother, Lance, the schoolteacher from Kingwilliamstown who did join up. There is also the third brother, the eldest, the one who lost the farm, but no one mentions him except his mother. 'Poor Roland,' murmurs his mother, shaking her head. Roland married a woman who calls herself Rosa Rakosta, daughter of an exiled Polish count, but whose real name, according to Norman, is Sophie Pretorius. Norman and Lance hate Roland because of the farm and despise him because he is under the thumb of Sophie. Roland and Sophie keep a boarding-house in Cape Town. He went there once, with his mother. Sophie turned out to be a large, fat blonde woman who wore a satin dressing-gown at four in the afternoon and smoked cigarettes in a cigarette-holder, Roland a quiet, sad-faced man with a bulbous red nose from the radium treatment that had cured him of cancer.

He likes it when his father and his mother and Norman get into political arguments. He enjoys the heat and passion, the reckless things they say. He is surprised that his father, the one he least wants to win, is the one he agrees with: that the English were good and the Germans bad, that Smuts was good and the Nats are bad.

His father likes the United Party, his father likes cricket and rugby, yet he does not like his father. He does not understand this contradiction, but has no interest in understanding it. Even before he knew his father, that is to say, before his father returned from the war, he had decided he was not going to like him. In a sense, therefore, the dislike is an abstract one: he does not want to have a father, or at least does not want a father who stays in the same house.

What he hates most about his father are his personal habits. He hates them so much that the mere thought of them makes him shudder with distaste: the loud nose-blowing in the bathroom in the mornings, the steamy smell of Lifebuoy soap that he leaves behind, along with a ring of scum and shaving-hairs in the washbasin. Most of all he hates the way his father smells. On the other hand, he likes, despite himself, his father's natty clothes, the maroon cravat he wears instead of a tie on Saturday mornings, his trim figure, his brisk way of walking, his Brylcreemed hair. He Brylcreems his own hair, cultivates a quiff.

He dislikes visiting the barber, dislikes it so much that he even tries, with embarrassing results, to cut his own hair. The barbers of Worcester seem to have decided in concert that boys should have short hair. Sessions begin as brutally as possible with the electric trimmer scything his hair away on the back and sides, and continue with a remorseless snick-snack of scissors till there is only a brush-like stubble left, with perhaps a saving cowlick at the front. Even before the session ends he is squirming with shame; he pays his shilling and hurries home, dreading school the next day, dreading the ritual jeers that greet every boy with a fresh haircut. There are proper haircuts and then there are the haircuts one suffers in Worcester, charged with the barbers' vindictiveness; he does not know where one has to go, what one has to do or say, how much one has to pay, to get a proper haircut.

SIX

THOUGH HE GOES to the bioscope every Saturday afternoon, films no longer have the hold on him that they had in Cape Town, where he had nightmares of being crushed under elevators or falling from cliffs like the heroes of the serials. He does not see why Errol Flynn, who looks just the same whether he is playing Robin Hood or Ali Baba, is supposed to be a great actor. He is tired of horseback chases, which are all the same. The Three Stooges have begun to seem silly. And it is hard to believe in Tarzan when the man who plays Tarzan keeps changing. The only film that makes an impression on him is one in which Ingrid Bergman gets into a train carriage that is infected with smallpox and dies. Ingrid Bergman is his mother's favourite actress. Is life like that: could his mother die at any moment just by failing to read a sign in a window?

There is also the radio. He has outgrown Children's Corner, but is faithful to the serials: Superman at 5.00 daily ('Up! Up and away!'), Mandrake the Magician at 5.30. His favourite story is 'The Snow-Goose' by Paul Gallico, which the A Service broadcasts again and again, by popular request. It is the story of a wild goose that leads the boats back from the beaches of Dunkirk to Dover. He listens with tears in his eyes. He wants one day to be faithful as the snow-goose is faithful.

They perform *Treasure Island* on the radio in a dramatized version, one half-hour episode a week. He has his own copy of *Treasure Island*; but he read it when he was too young, not understanding the business of the blind man and the black spot, unable to work out whether Long John Silver was good or bad. Now, after every episode on the radio, he has nightmares centring on Long John: about the crutch with which he kills people, about his treacherous, sentimental solicitude for Jim Hawkins. He wishes Squire Trelawney would kill Long John instead of letting him go: he is sure he will return one day with his cutthroat mutineers to take his revenge, just as he returns in his dreams.

The Swiss Family Robinson is much more comforting. He has a handsome copy of the book with colour plates. He particularly likes the picture of the ship in its cradle under the trees, the ship that the family has built with tools salvaged from the wreck, to take them back home with all their animals, like Noah's Ark. It is a pleasure, like slipping into a warm bath, to leave Treasure Island behind and enter the world of the Swiss Family. In the Swiss Family there are no bad brothers, no murderous pirates; in their family everyone works happily together under the guidance of a wise, strong father (the pictures show him with a barrel chest and a long chestnut beard) who knows from the beginning what needs to be done to save them. The only thing that puzzles him is why, when they are so snug and happy on the island, they have to leave at all.

He owns a third book too, *Scott of the Antarctic*. Captain Scott is one of his unquestioned heroes: that is why the book was given to him. It has photographs, including one of Scott sitting and writing in the tent in which he later froze to death. He often looks at the photographs, but he does not get far with reading the book: it is boring, it is not a story. He only likes the bit about Titus Oates, the man with frostbite who, because he was holding up his companions, went out into the night, into the snow and ice, and perished quietly, without fuss. He hopes he can be like Titus Oates one day.

Once a year Boswell's Circus comes to Worcester. Everyone in his class goes; for a week talk is about the circus and nothing else. Even the Coloured children go, after a fashion: they hang around outside the tent for hours, listening to the band, peering in through gaps.

They plan to go on the Saturday afternoon, when his father is playing cricket. His mother makes it into an outing for the three of them. But at the ticket booth she hears with a shock the high Saturday afternoon prices: 2/6 for children, 5/- for adults. She does not have enough money with her. She buys tickets for him and his brother. 'Go in, I'll wait here,' she says. He is unwilling, but she insists.

Inside, he is miserable, enjoys nothing; he suspects his brother feels the same way. When they emerge at the end of the show, she is still there. For days afterwards he cannot banish the thought: his mother waiting patiently in the blazing heat of December while he sits in the circus tent being entertained like a king. Her blinding, overwhelming, self-sacrificial love, for both him and his brother but for him in particular, disturbs him. He wishes she did not love him so much. She loves him absolutely, therefore he must love her absolutely: that is the logic she compels upon him. Never will he be able to pay back all the love she pours out upon him. The thought of a lifetime bowed under a debt of love baffles and infuriates him to the point where he will not kiss her, refuses to be touched by her. When she turns away in silent hurt, he deliberately hardens his heart against her, refusing to give in.

Sometimes, when she is feeling bitter, she makes long speeches to herself, contrasting her life on the barren housing estate with the life she lived before she was married, which she represents as a continual round of parties and picnics, of week-end visits to farms, of tennis and golf and walks with her dogs. She speaks in a low whispering voice in which only the sibilants stand out: he in his room, and his brother in his, strain their ears to hear, as she must know they will. That is another reason why his father calls her a witch: because she talks to herself, making up spells.

The idyll of life in Victoria West is substantiated by photographs from the albums: his mother, together with other women in long white dresses, standing with tennis racquets in what looks like the middle of the veld, his mother with her arm over the neck of a dog, an Alsatian.

'Was that your dog?' he asks.

'That is Kim. He was the best, the most faithful dog I ever had.'

'What happened to him?'

'He ate poisoned meat that the farmers had put down for jackals. He died in my arms.'

There are tears in her eyes.

After his father makes his appearance in the album there are no more dogs. Instead he sees the two of them at picnics with their friends from those days, or his father, with his dapper little moustache and his cocky look, posing against the bonnet of an old-fashioned black car. Then the pictures of himself begin, dozens of them, starting with the picture of a blank-faced, pudgy baby being held up to the camera by a dark, intense-looking woman.

In all these photographs, even the photographs with the baby, his mother strikes him as girlish. Her age is a mystery that intrigues him endlessly. She will not tell him, his father pretends not to know, even her brothers and sisters seem sworn to secrecy. While she is out of the house he searches through the papers in the bottom drawer of her dressing-table, looking for a birth certificate, but without success. From a remark she has let slip he knows she is older than his father, who was born in 1912; but how much older? He decides she was born in 1910. That means she was thirty when he was born and is forty now. 'You're forty!' he tells her triumphantly one day, watching closely for signs that he is right. She gives a mysterious smile. 'I'm twenty-eight,' she says.

They have the same birthday. He was born to her on her birthday. This means, as she has told him, as she tells everyone, that he is a gift of God.

He calls her not Mother or Mom but Dinny. So do his father and his brother. Where does the name come from? No one seems to know; but her brothers and sisters call her Vera, so it cannot come from their childhood. He has to be careful not to call her Dinny in front of strangers, as he has to guard against calling his aunt and uncle plain Norman and Ellen instead of Uncle Norman and Aunt Ellen. But saying Uncle and Aunt like a good, obedient, normal child is as nothing beside the circumlocutions of Afrikaans. Afrikaners are afraid to say *you* to anyone older than themselves. He mocks his father's speech: *'Mammie moet 'n kombers oor Mammie se knieë trek anders word Mammie koud'*—Mommy must put a blanket over Mommy's knees, otherwise Mommy will get cold. He is relieved he is not Afrikaans and is saved from having to talk like that, like a whipped slave.

HIS MOTHER DECIDES that she wants a dog. Alsatians are the best—the most intelligent, the most faithful—but they cannot find an Alsatian for sale. So they settle for a pup half Doberman, half something else. He insists on being the one to name it. He would like to call it Borzoi because he wants it to be a Russian dog, but since it is not in fact a borzoi he calls it Cossack. No one understands. People think the name is *kos-sak*, food-bag, which they find funny.

Cossack turns out to be a confused, undisciplined dog, roaming about the neighbourhood, trampling gardens, chasing chickens. One day the dog follows him all the way to school. Nothing he does will put him off: when he shouts and throws stones the dog drops his ears, puts his tail between his legs, slinks away; but as soon as he gets back on his bicycle the dog lopes after him again. In the end he has to drag him home by the collar, pushing his bicycle with the other hand. He gets home in a rage and refuses to go back to school, since he is late.

Cossack is not quite full grown when he eats the ground glass someone has put out for him. His mother administers enemas, trying to flush out the glass, but without success. On the third day, when the dog just lies still, panting, and will not even lick her hand, she sends him to the pharmacy to fetch a new medicine someone has recommended. He races there and races back, but he comes too late. His mother's face is drawn and remote, she will not even take the bottle from his hands.

He helps to bury Cossack, wrapped in a blanket, in the clay at the bottom of the garden. Over the grave he erects a cross with the name 'Cossack' painted on it. He does not want them to have another dog, not if this is how they must die.

HIS FATHER PLAYS CRICKET for Worcester. It ought to be yet another feather in his cap, another source of pride for him. His father is an attorney, which is almost as good as a doctor; he was a soldier in the war; he used to play rugby in the Cape Town league; he plays cricket. But in each case there is an embarrassing qualification. He is an attorney but no longer practises. He was a soldier but only a lance-corporal. He played rugby, but only for Gardens second team, and Gardens are a joke, they always come bottom of the Grand Challenge league. And now he plays cricket, but for the Worcester second team, which no one bothers to watch.

His father is a bowler, not a batsman. There is something wrong with his backlift that bedevils his batting; furthermore, he averts his eyes when he plays fast bowling. His idea of batting seems to be confined to pushing the bat forward and, if the ball slides off it, trotting a sedate single.

The reason why his father can't bat is of course that he grew up in the Karoo, where there was no proper cricket and no way of learning. Bowling is a different matter. It is a gift: bowlers are born, not made.

His father bowls slow off-spinners. Sometimes he is hit for six; sometimes, seeing the ball slowly floating towards him, the batsman loses his head, swings wildly, and is bowled. That seems to be his father's method: patience, cunning.

The coach for the Worcester teams is Johnny Wardle, who in the northern summer plays cricket for England. It is a great coup for Worcester that Johnny Wardle has chosen to come here. Wolf Heller is mentioned as an intercessor, Wolf Heller and his money.

He stands with his father behind the practice net watching Johnny Wardle bowl to the first-team batsmen. Wardle, a nondescript little man with sparse sandy hair, is supposed to be a slow bowler, but when he trots up and releases the ball he is surprised at how fast it travels. The batsman at the crease plays the ball easily enough, stroking it gently into the netting. Someone else bowls, then it is Wardle's turn again. Again the batsman strokes the ball gently away. The batsman is not winning, but neither is the bowler.

At the end of the afternoon he goes home disappointed. He had expected more of a gulf between the England bowler and the Worcester batsmen. He had expected to be witness to a more mysterious craft, to see the ball doing strange things in the air and off the pitch, floating and dipping and spinning, as great slow bowling is supposed to do according to the cricket books he reads. He was not expecting a talkative little man whose only mark of distinction is that he bowls spinners as fast as he himself bowls at his fastest.

To cricket he looks for more than Johnny Wardle offers. Cricket must be like Horatius and the Etruscans, or Hector and Achilles. If Hector and Achilles were just two men hacking away at each other with swords, there would be no point to the story. But they are not just two men: they are mighty heroes, their names ring in legend. He is glad when, at the end of the season, Wardle is dropped from the England team.

Wardle bowls, of course, with a leather ball. He is unfamiliar with the leather ball: he and his friends play with what they call a cork ball, compacted out of some hard, grey material that is proof against the stones that tear the stitching of a leather ball to shreds. Standing behind the net watching Wardle, he hears for the first time the strange whistling of a leather ball as it approaches the batsman through the air.

His first chance comes to play on a proper cricket field. A match is organized for a Wednesday afternoon, between two teams from the junior school. Proper cricket means proper wickets, a proper pitch, no need to fight for a turn to bat.

His turn comes to bat. Wearing a pad on his left leg, carrying his father's bat that is much too heavy for him, he walks out to the middle. He is surprised at how big the field is. It is a great and lonely place: the spectators are so far away that they might as well not exist.

He takes his stand on the strip of rolled earth with a green coir mat spread over it and waits for the ball to come. This is cricket. It is called a game, but it feels to him more real than home, more real even than school. In this game there is no pretending, no mercy, no second chance. These other boys, whose names he does not know, are all against him. They are of one mind only: to cut short his pleasure. They will feel not one speck of remorse when he is out. In the middle of this huge arena he is on trial, one against eleven, with no one to protect him.

The fielders settle into position. He must concentrate, but there is something irritating he cannot put out of his mind: Zeno's paradox. Before the arrow can reach its target it must reach half-way; before it can reach half-way it must reach a quarter of the way; before it can reach a quarter of the way . . . Desperately he tries to stop thinking about it; but the very fact that he is trying not to think about it agitates him still further.

The bowler runs up. He hears particularly the thud of the last two steps. Then there is a space in which the only sound breaking the silence is the eerie rustling noise of the ball as it tumbles and dips towards him. Is this what he is choosing when he chooses to play cricket: to be tested again and again and again, until he fails, by a ball that comes at him impersonally, indifferently, without mercy, seeking the chink in his defence, and faster than he expects, too fast for him to clear the confusion in his mind, compose his thoughts, decide properly what to do? And in the midst of this thinking, in the midst of this muddle, the ball arrives.

He scores two runs, batting in a state of disarray and, later, of gloom. He emerges from the game understanding less than ever the matter-of-fact way in which Johnny Wardle plays, chatting and joking all the while. Are all the fabled England players like that: Len Hutton, Alec Bedser, Denis Compton, Cyril Washbrook? He cannot believe it. To him, real cricket can only be played in silence, silence and apprehension, the heart thudding in the chest, the mouth dry.

Cricket is not a game. It is the truth of life. If it is, as the books say, a test of character, then it is a test he sees no way of passing yet does not know how to dodge. At the wicket the secret that he manages to cover up elsewhere is relentlessly probed and exposed. 'Let us see what you are made of,' says the ball as it whistles and tumbles through the air toward him. Blindly, confusedly, he pushes the bat forward, too soon or too late. Past the bat, past the pads the ball finds its way. He is bowled, he has failed the test, he has been found out, there is nothing to do but hide his tears, cover his face, trudge back to the commiserating, politely schooled applause of the other boys.

SEVEN

ON HIS BICYCLE is the British Small Arms emblem of two crossed rifles and the label 'Smiths—BSA'. He bought the bicycle for five pounds, second-hand, with the money for his eighth birthday. It is the most solid thing in his life. When other boys boast that they have Raleighs, he replies that he has a Smiths. 'Smiths? Never heard of Smiths,' they say.

There is nothing to match the elation of riding a bicycle, of leaning over and swooping through the curves. On his Smiths he rides to school every morning, the half-mile from Reunion Park to the railway crossing, then the mile on the quiet road alongside the railway line. Summer mornings are the best. Water murmurs in the roadside furrows, doves coo in the bluegum trees; now and then there is an eddy of warm air to warn of the wind that will blow later in the day, chasing gusts of fine red clay-dust before it.

In winter he has to set out for school while it is still dark. With his lamp casting a halo before him, he rides through the mist, breasting its velvety softness, breathing it in, breathing it out, hearing nothing but the soft swish of his tyres. Some mornings the metal of the handlebars is so cold that his bare hands stick to it.

He tries to get to school early. He loves to have the classroom to himself, to wander around the empty seats, to mount, surreptitiously, the teacher's podium. But he is never first at school: there are two brothers from De Doorns whose father works on the railways and who come in on the 6 A.M. train. They are poor, so poor that they own neither jerseys nor blazers nor shoes. There are other boys just as poor, particularly in the Afrikaans classes. Even on icy winter mornings they come to school in thin cotton shirts and serge short-pants so outgrown that their slim thighs can hardly move in them. Their tanned legs show chalk-white patches of cold; they blow on their hands and stamp their feet; snot is always running out of their noses.

Once there is an outbreak of ringworm, and the brothers from De Doorns have their heads shaved. On their bare skulls he can clearly see the whorls of the ringworm; his mother warns him to have no contact with them.

He prefers tight shorts to loose shorts. The clothes his mother buys for him are always too loose. He likes to gaze at slim, smooth brown legs in tight shorts. Best of all he loves the honey-tan legs of boys with blond hair. The most beautiful boys, he is surprised to find, are in the Afrikaans classes, as are the ugliest, the ones with hairy legs and Adam's apples and pustules on their faces. Afrikaans children are almost like Coloured children, he finds, unspoiled and thoughtless, running wild, then suddenly, at a certain age, going bad, their beauty dying within them.

Beauty and desire: he is disturbed by the feelings that the legs of these boys, blank and perfect and inexpressive, create in him. What is there that can be done with legs beyond devouring them with one's eyes? What is desire *for*?

The naked sculptures in the *Children's Encyclopaedia* affect him in the same way: Daphne pursued by Apollo; Persephone ravished by Dis. It is a matter of shape, of perfection of shape.

He has an idea of the perfect human body. When he sees that perfection manifested in white marble, something thrills inside him; a gulf opens up; he is on the edge of falling.

Of all the secrets that set him apart, this may in the end be the worst. Among all these boys he is the only one in whom this dark erotic current runs; among all this innocence and normality, he is the only one who desires.

Yet the language of the Afrikaans boys is filthy beyond belief. They command a range of obscenity far beyond his, to do with *fok* and *piel* and *poes*, words from whose monosyllabic heaviness he retreats in dismay. How are they written? Until he can write them he has no way of taming them in his mind. Is *fok* spelled with a *v*, which would make it more venerable, or with an *f*, which would make it a truly wild word, primeval, without ancestry? The dictionary says nothing, the words are not there, none of them.

Then there are *gat* and *poep-hol* and words like them, hurled back and forth in bouts of abuse whose force he does not understand. Why couple the back of the body with the front? What have the *gat*-words, so heavy and guttural and black, to do with sex, with its softly inviting *s* and its mysterious final *x*? He shuts his mind to the backside-words in distaste but continues to try to puzzle out the meaning of *effies* and *FLs*, things he has never seen but that belong, somehow, to the commerce of boys and girls in high school.

Yet he is not ignorant. He knows how babies are born. They come out of the mother's backside, neat and clean and white. So his mother told him years ago, when he was small. He believes her without question: it is a source of pride to him that she told him the truth about babies so early, when other children were still being fobbed off with lies. It is a mark of her enlightenment, of their family's enlightenment. His cousin Juan, who is a year younger than he, knows the truth too. His father, on the other hand, gets embarrassed and grumbles when there is talk of babies and where they come from; but that just proves once again the benightedness of his father's family.

His friends hold to a different story: that babies come out of the other hole.

He knows in the abstract of another hole, into which the penis goes and out of which the urine comes. But it makes no sense that the baby comes out of that hole. The baby is, after all, formed in the stomach. So it makes sense for the baby to come out of the backside.

Therefore he argues for the backside while his friends argue for the other hole, the *poes*. He is quietly convinced he is right. It is part of the trust between his mother and himself.

EIGHT

HE AND HIS MOTHER are crossing a strip of public ground near the railway station. He is with her but separate from her, not holding her hand. He is, as ever, wearing grey: grey jersey, grey shorts, grey stockings. On his head is a navy-blue cap with the badge of Worcester Boys Primary School: a mountain peak surrounded by stars, and the legend PER ASPERA AD ASTRA.

He is just a boy walking beside his mother: from the outside he probably looks quite normal. But he thinks of himself as scuttling around her like a beetle, scuttling in fussy circles with his nose to the ground and his legs and arms pumping. In fact he can think of nothing about himself that is still. His mind in particular darts about here and there all the time, with an impatient will of its own.

This is the place where once a year the circus pitches its tent and parks cages in which lions drowse in their smelly straw. But today it is just a patch of red clay packed hard as rock, where grass will not grow.

There are other people too, other passers-by, on this bright, hot Saturday morning. One of them is a boy of his own age trotting across the square at an angle to them. And as soon as he sees him, he knows that this boy will be important to him, important beyond all measure, not because of who he is (he may never see him again) but because of the thoughts that are going on in his head, that burst out of him like a swarm of bees.

There is nothing unusual about the boy. He is Coloured, but there are Coloured people everywhere. He is wearing pants so short that they sit tightly across his neat buttocks and leave his slim clay-brown thighs almost naked. He wears no shoes; his soles are probably so hard that even if he trod on a *duwweltjie* thorn he would merely check his stride, reach down, brush it away.

There are hundreds of boys like him, thousands, thousands of girls too in short frocks that show off their slim legs. He wishes he had legs as beautiful as theirs. With legs like that he would float across the earth as this boy does, barely touching it.

The boy passes within a dozen paces of them. He is absorbed in himself, he does not glance at them. His body is perfect and unspoiled, as if it had emerged only yesterday from its shell. Why do children like this, boys and girls under no compulsion to go to school, free to roam far from the watching eyes of parents, whose bodies are their own to do with as they please—why do they not come together in a feast of sexual delight? Is the answer that they are too innocent to know what pleasures are available to them—that only dark and guilty souls know such secrets?

That is how the questioning always works. At first it may wander here and there; but in the end, unfailingly, it turns and gathers itself and points a finger at himself. Always it is he who sets the train of thinking in motion; always it is the thinking that slips out of his control and returns to accuse him. Beauty is innocence; innocence is ignorance; ignorance is ignorance of pleasure; pleasure is guilty; he is guilty. This boy, with his fresh, untouched body, is innocent, while he, ruled by his dark desires, is guilty. In fact, by this long path he has come within

sight of the word *perversion,* with its dark, complex thrill, beginning with the enigmatic *p* that can mean anything, then swiftly
tumbling via the ruthless *r* to the vengeful *v.* Not one accusation
but two. The two accusations cross, and he is at their point of
crossing, in the gunsight. For the one who brings the accusation
to bear on him today is not only light as a deer and innocent
while he is dark and heavy and guilty: he is also Coloured,
which means that he has no money, lives in an obscure hovel,
goes hungry; it means that if his mother were to call out
'Boy!' and wave, as she is quite capable of doing, this boy would
have to stop in his tracks and come and do whatever she might
tell him (carry her shopping basket, for instance), and at the end
of it get a tickey in his cupped hands and be grateful for it. And
if he were to be angry with his mother afterwards, she would
simply smile and say, 'But they are used to it!'

So this boy who has unreflectingly kept all his life to the path
of nature and innocence, who is poor and therefore good, as the
poor always are in fairy-tales, who is slim as an eel and quick as
a hare and would defeat him with ease in any contest of swift-
ness of foot or skill of hand—this boy, who is a living reproof to
him, is nevertheless subjected to him in ways that embarrass
him so much that he squirms and wriggles his shoulders and
does not want to look at him any longer, despite his beauty.

Yet one cannot dismiss him. One can dismiss the Natives,
perhaps, but one cannot dismiss the Coloured people. The Natives can be argued away because they are latecomers, invaders
from the north, and have no right to be here. The Natives one
sees in Worcester are, for the most part, men dressed in old
army coats, smoking hooked pipes, who live in tiny tent-shaped
corrugated-iron kennels along the railway line, men whose
strength and patience are legendary. They have been brought
here because they do not drink, as Coloured men do, because

they can do heavy labour under a blazing sun where lighter, more volatile Coloured men would collapse. They are men without women, without children, who arrive from nowhere and can be made to disappear into nowhere.

But against the Coloureds there is no such recourse. The Coloureds were fathered by the whites, by Jan van Riebeeck, upon the Hottentots: that much is plain, even in the veiled language of his school history book. In a bitter way it is even worse than that. For in the Boland the people called Coloured are not the great-great-grandchildren of Jan van Riebeeck or any other Dutchman. He is expert enough in physiognomy, has been expert enough as long as he can remember, to know that there is not a drop of white blood in them. They are Hottentots, pure and uncorrupted. Not only do they come with the land, the land comes with them, is theirs, has always been.

NINE

ONE OF THE CONVENIENCES of Worcester, one of the reasons, according to his father, why it is better living here than in Cape Town, is that shopping is so much easier. Milk is delivered every morning before dawn; one has only to pick up the telephone and, an hour or two later, the man from Schochat's will be at the door with one's meat and groceries. It is as simple as that.

The man from Schochat's, the delivery boy, is a Native who speaks only a few words of Afrikaans and no English. He wears a clean white shirt, a bow-tie, two-tone shoes, and a Bobby Locke cap. His name is Josias. His parents disapprove of him as one of the feckless new generation of Natives who spend all their pay on fancy clothes and give no thought to the future.

When his mother is not at home, he and his brother receive the order from Josias, packing the groceries away on the kitchen shelf and the meat in the refrigerator. If there is condensed milk, they appropriate it as booty. They punch holes in the can and take turns sucking till it is dry. When their mother comes home they pretend that there was no condensed milk, or that Josias stole it.

Whether she believes their lie he is not sure. But this is not a deceit he feels particularly guilty about.

The neighbours on the east side are named Wynstra. They

have three sons, an older one with knock knees named Gysbert and twins named Eben and Ezer too young to go to school. He and his brother ridicule Gysbert Wynstra for his funny name and for the soft, helpless way in which he runs. They decide he is an idiot, mentally deficient, and declare war on him. One afternoon they take the half-dozen eggs Schochat's boy has delivered, hurl them at the roof of the Wynstra house, and hide. The Wynstras do not emerge, but, as the sun dries the smashed eggs, they turn to ugly splashes of yellow.

The pleasure of throwing an egg, so much smaller and lighter than a cricket ball, of watching it fly through the air, end over end, of hearing the soft crunch of its impact, remains with him long afterwards. Yet his pleasure is tinged with guilt. He cannot forget that it is food they are playing with. By what right does he use eggs as playthings? What would Schochat's boy say if he found they were throwing away the eggs he had brought all the way from town on his bicycle? He has a sense that Schochat's boy, who is in fact not a boy at all but a grown man, would not be so wrapped up in the image of himself in his Bobby Locke cap and bow-tie as to be indifferent. He has a sense that he would disapprove most strongly and would not hesitate to say so. 'How can you do that when children are hungry?' he would say in his bad Afrikaans; and there would be no answer. Perhaps elsewhere in the world one can throw eggs (in England, for instance, he knows they throw eggs at people in the stocks); but in this country there are judges who will judge by the standards of righteousness. In this country one cannot be thoughtless about food.

Josias is the fourth Native he has known in his life. The first, whom he remembers only dimly as wearing blue pyjamas all day long, was the boy who used to mop the stairs of the block of flats they lived in in Johannesburg. The second was Fiela in Plettenberg Bay, who took in their washing. Fiela was very black and very old and had no teeth and made long speeches about the past in beautiful, rolling English. She came from St Helena, she said, where she had been a slave. The third was also in Plettenberg Bay. There had been a great storm; a ship had sunk; the wind, which had blown for days and nights, was just beginning to die down. He and his mother and his brother were out on the beach inspecting the mounds of jetsam and seaweed that had been washed up, when an old man with a grey beard and a clerical collar, carrying an umbrella, came up to them and addressed them. 'Man builds great boats of iron,' said the old man, 'but the sea is stronger. The sea is stronger than anything man can build.'

When they were alone again, his mother had said: 'You must remember what he said. He was a wise old man.' It is the only time he can remember her using the word *wise*; in fact it is the only time he can remember anyone using the word outside of books. But it is not just the old-fashioned word that impresses him. It is possible to respect Natives—that is what she is saying. It is a great relief to hear that, to have it confirmed.

In the stories that have left the deepest mark on him, it is the third brother, the humblest and most derided, who, after the first and second brothers have disdainfully passed by, helps the old woman to carry her heavy load or draws the thorn from the lion's paw. The third brother is kind and honest and courageous while the first and second brothers are boastful, arrogant, uncharitable. At the end of the story the third brother is crowned prince, while the first and second brothers are disgraced and sent packing.

There are white people and Coloured people and Natives, of whom the Natives are the lowest and most derided. The parallel is inescapable: the Natives are the third brother.

At school they learn, over and over again, year after year,

about Jan van Riebeeck and Simon van der Stel and Lord Charles Somerset and Piet Retief. After Piet Retief come the Kaffir Wars, when the Kaffirs poured over the borders of the Colony and had to be driven back; but the Kaffir Wars are so many and so confused and so hard to keep apart that they are not required to know them for examinations.

Although, in examinations, he gives the correct answers to the history questions, he does not know, in a way that satisfies his heart, why Jan van Riebeeck and Simon van der Stel were so good while Lord Charles Somerset was so bad. Nor does he like the leaders of the Great Trek as he is supposed to, except perhaps for Piet Retief, who was murdered after Dingaan tricked him into leaving his gun outside the kraal. Andries Pretorius and Gerrit Maritz and the others sound like the teachers in the high school or like Afrikaners on the radio: angry and obdurate and full of menaces and talk about God.

They do not cover the Boer War at school, at least not in English-medium classes. There are rumours that the Boer War is taught in the Afrikaans classes, under the name of the Tweede Vryheidsoorlog, the Second War of Liberation, but not for examination. Being a touchy subject, the Boer War is not officially on the syllabus. Even his parents will not say anything about the Boer War, about who was right and who was wrong. However, his mother does repeat a story about the Boer War that her own mother told her. When the Boers arrived on their farm, said her mother, they demanded food and money and expected to be waited on. When the British soldiers came, they slept in the stable, stole nothing, and before leaving courteously thanked their hosts.

The British, with their haughty, arrogant generals, are the villains of the Boer War. They are also stupid, for wearing red uniforms that make them easy targets for the Boer marksmen. In stories of the War one is supposed to side with the Boers, fighting for their freedom against the might of the British Empire. However, he prefers to dislike the Boers, not only for their long beards and ugly clothes, but for hiding behind rocks and shooting from ambush, and to like the British for marching to their death to the skirl of bagpipes.

In Worcester the English are a minority, in Reunion Park a tiny minority. Aside from himself and his brother, who are English only in a way, there are only two English boys: Rob Hart and a small, wiry boy named Billy Smith whose father works on the railways and who has a sickness that makes his skin flake off (his mother forbids him to touch any of the Smith children).

When he lets it slip that Rob Hart is being flogged by Miss Oosthuizen, his parents seem at once to know why. Miss Oosthuizen is one of the Oosthuizen clan, who are Nationalists; Rob Hart's father, who owns a hardware store, was a United Party town councillor until the elections of 1948.

His parents shake their heads over Miss Oosthuizen. They regard her as excitable, unstable; they disapprove of her hennaed hair. Under Smuts, his father says, something would have been done about a teacher who brought politics into school. His father is also United Party. In fact his father lost his job in Cape Town, the job with the title his mother was so proud of—Controller of Letting—when Malan beat Smuts in 1948. It was because of Malan that they had to leave the house in Rosebank that he looks back on with such longing, the house with the big overgrown garden and the observatory with the domed roof and the two cellars, had to leave Rosebank Junior School and his Rosebank friends, and come here to Worcester. In Cape Town his father used to set off to work in the mornings wearing a dapper double-breasted suit, carrying a leather attaché case. When other children asked what his father did, he could reply, 'He is

Controller of Letting,' and they would fall respectfully silent. In Worcester his father's work has no name. 'My father works for Standard Canners,' he has to say. 'But what does he do?' 'He is in the office, he keeps the books,' he has to say, lamely. He has no idea what 'keeping books' means.

Standard Canners produces canned Alberta peaches, canned Bartlett pears and canned apricots. Standard Canners cans more peaches than any other canner in the country: that is all it is famous for.

Despite the defeat of 1948 and the death of General Smuts, his father remains loyal to the United Party: loyal but gloomy. Advocate Strauss, the new leader of the United Party, is only a pale shadow of Smuts; under Strauss the UP has no hope of winning the next election. Furthermore, the Nats are assuring themselves of victory by redrawing the boundaries of constituencies to favour their supporters in the *platteland,* the countryside.

'Why don't they do something about it?' he asks his father.

'Who?' says his father. 'Who can stop them? They can do what they like, now that they are in power.'

He does not see the point of having elections if the party that wins can change the rules. It is like the batsman deciding who may and who may not bowl.

His father switches on the radio at news-time but really only to listen to the scores, cricket scores in the summer, rugby scores in the winter.

The news bulletin used once to come from England, before the Nats took over. First there would be 'God Save the King,' then there would be the six pips from Greenwich, then the announcer would say, 'This is London, here is the news,' and read news from all over the world. Now all that is finished. 'This is the South African Broadcasting Corporation,' says the announcer, and plunges into a long recital of what Dr Malan said in Parliament.

What he hates most about Worcester, what most makes him want to escape, is the rage and resentment that he senses crackling through the Afrikaans boys. He fears and loathes the hulking, barefoot Afrikaans boys in their tight short trousers, particularly the older boys, who, given half a chance, will take you off to some quiet place in the veld and violate you in ways he has heard leeringly alluded to—*borsel* you, for instance, which as far as he can work out means pulling down your pants and brushing shoe-polish into your balls (but why your balls? why shoe-polish?) and sending you home through the streets half-naked and blubbering.

There is a lore that all Afrikaans boys seem to share, spread by the student teachers who visit the school, to do with initiation and what happens to you during initiation. The Afrikaans boys whisper about it in the same excited way that they talk of being caned. What he overhears repels him: walking around in a baby's nappie, for instance, or drinking urine. If that is what you have to go through before you can become a teacher, he refuses to become a teacher.

There are rumours that the Government is going to order all schoolchildren with Afrikaans surnames to be transferred to Afrikaans classes. His parents talk about it in low voices; they are clearly worried. As for him, he is filled with panic at the thought of having to move to an Afrikaans class. He tells his parents he will not obey. He will refuse to go to school. They try to calm him. 'Nothing will happen,' they say. 'It is just talk. It will be years before they do anything.' He is not reassured.

It will be up to the school inspectors, he learns, to remove false English boys from the English classes. He lives in dread of the day when the inspector will come, run his finger down the register, call out his name, and tell him to pack his books. He has a plan for that day, carefully worked out. He will pack his books and leave the room without protest. But he will not go to the Afrikaans class. Instead, calmly, so as not to attract attention, he will walk over to the bicycle shed, take his bicycle, and ride home so fast that no one can catch him. Then he will close and lock the front door and tell his mother that he is not going back to school, that if she betrays him he will kill himself.

An image of Dr Malan is engraved in his mind. Dr Malan's round, bald face is without understanding or mercy. His gullet pulses like a frog's. His lips are pursed.

He has not forgotten Dr Malan's first act in 1948: to ban all Captain Marvel and Superman comics, allowing only comics with animal characters, comics intended to keep one a baby, to pass through the Customs.

He thinks of the Afrikaans songs they are made to sing at school. He has come to hate them so much that he wants to scream and shout and make farting noises during the singing, particularly during *'Kom ons gaan blomme pluk,'* with its children gambolling in the fields among chirping birds and jolly insects.

One Saturday morning he and two friends cycle out of Worcester along the De Doorns road. In half an hour they are out of sight of human habitation. They leave their bicycles at the roadside and strike off into the hills. They find a cave, make a fire, and eat the sandwiches they have brought. Suddenly a huge, truculent Afrikaans boy in khaki shorts appears. *'Wie het julle toestemming gegee?'*—Who gave you permission?

They are struck dumb. A cave: do they need permission to be in a cave? They try to make up lies, but it is no use. *'Julle sal hier moet bly totdat my pa kom,'* the boy announces: You will have to wait here till my father comes. He mentions a *lat*, a *strop*: a cane, a strap; they are going to be taught a lesson.

He grows light-headed with fear. Here, out in the veld where there is no one to call to, they are going to be beaten. There is no appeal they can make. For the fact is, they are guilty, he most of all. He was the one who assured the others, when they climbed through the fence, that it could not be a farm, it was just veld. He is the ringleader, it was his idea from the beginning, there is no one else on to whom the blame can be shifted.

The farmer arrives with his dog, a sly-looking, yellow-eyed Alsatian. Again the questions, this time in English, questions without answers. By what right are they here? Why did they not ask permission? Again the pathetic, stupid defence must be gone through: they did not know, they thought it was just veld. To himself he swears he will never make the same mistake again. Never again will he be so stupid as to climb through a fence and think he can get away with it. *Stupid!* he thinks to himself: *stupid, stupid, stupid!*

The farmer does not happen to have a *lat* or a strap or a whip with him. 'Your lucky day,' he says. They stand rooted to the spot, not understanding. 'Go.'

Stupidly they clamber down the hillside, careful not to run for fear the dog will come after them barking and slavering, to where their bicycles wait at the roadside. There is nothing they can say to redeem the experience. The Afrikaners have not even behaved badly. It is they who have lost.

TEN

IN THE EARLY MORNINGS there are Coloured children trotting along the National Road with pencil-cases and exercise books, some even with satchels on their backs, on their way to school. But they are young children, very young: by the time they are his age, ten or eleven, they will have left school behind and be out in the world earning their daily bread.

On his birthday, instead of a party, he is given ten shillings to take his friends for a treat. He invites his three best friends to the Globe Café; they sit at a marble-topped table and order banana splits or chocolate fudge sundaes. He feels princely, dispensing pleasure like this; the occasion would be a marvellous success, were it not spoiled by the ragged Coloured children standing at the window looking in on them.

On the faces of these children he sees none of the hatred which, he is prepared to acknowledge, he and his friends deserve for having so much money while they are penniless. On the contrary, they are like children at a circus, drinking in the sight, utterly absorbed, missing nothing.

If he were someone else, he would ask the Portuguese with the Brilliantined hair who owns the Globe to chase them away. It is quite normal to chase beggar children away. You have only to contort your face into a scowl and wave your arms and shout,

'*Voetsek, hotnot! Loop! Loop!*' and then turn to whoever is watching, friend or stranger, and explain: '*Hulle soek net iets om te steel. Hulle is almal skelms.*'—They are just looking for something to steal. They are all thieves. But if he were to get up and go to the Portuguese, what would he say? 'They are spoiling my birthday, it is not fair, it hurts my heart to see them'? Whatever happens, whether they are chased away or not, it is too late, his heart is already hurt.

He thinks of Afrikaners as people in a rage all the time because their hearts are hurt. He thinks of the English as people who have not fallen into a rage because they live behind walls and guard their hearts well.

This is only one of his theories about the English and the Afrikaners. The fly in the ointment, unfortunately, is Trevelyan.

Trevelyan was one of the lodgers who boarded with them in the house in Liesbeeck Road, Rosebank, the house with the great oak tree in the front garden where he was happy. Trevelyan had the best room, the one with French windows opening on to the stoep. He was young, he was tall, he was friendly, he could not speak a word of Afrikaans, he was English through and through. In the mornings Trevelyan had breakfast in the kitchen before going off to work; in the evenings he came back and had supper with them. He kept his room, which was anyhow out of bounds, locked; but there was nothing interesting in it except an electric shaver made in America.

His father, though older than Trevelyan, became Trevelyan's friend. On Saturdays they listened to the radio together, to C K Friedlander broadcasting rugby matches from Newlands.

Then Eddie arrived. Eddie was a seven-year-old Coloured boy from Ida's Valley near Stellenbosch. He came to work for them: the arrangement was made between Eddie's mother and Aunt Winnie, who lived in Stellenbosch. In return for washing dishes and sweeping and polishing, Eddie would live with them in Rosebank and be given his meals, while on the first of every month his mother would be sent a postal order for two pounds ten shillings.

After two months of living and working in Rosebank, Eddie ran away. He disappeared during the night; his absence was discovered in the morning. The police were called in; Eddie was found not far away, hiding in the bushes along the Liesbeeck River. He was found not by the police but by Trevelyan, who dragged him back, crying and kicking shamelessly, and locked him up in the old observatory in the back garden.

Obviously Eddie would have to be sent back to Ida's Valley. Now that he had dropped the pretence of being content, he would run away at every opportunity. Apprenticeship had not worked.

But before Aunt Winnie in Stellenbosch could be telephoned there was the question of punishment for the trouble Eddie had caused: for the calling in of the police, for the ruined Saturday morning. It was Trevelyan who offered to carry out the punishment.

He peered into the observatory once while it was going on. Trevelyan was holding Eddie by the two wrists and flogging him on the bare legs with a leather strap. His father was also there, standing to one side, watching. Eddie howled and danced; there were tears and snot everywhere. *'Asseblief, asseblief, my baas,'* he howled, *'ek sal nie weer nie!'*—I won't do it again! Then the two of them noticed him and waved him out.

The next day his aunt and uncle came from Stellenbosch in their black DKW to take Eddie back to his mother in Ida's Valley. There were no goodbyes.

So Trevelyan, who was English, was the one to beat Eddie. In fact, Trevelyan, who was ruddy of complexion and already a little fat, went even ruddier while he was applying the strap, and snorted with every blow, working himself into as much of a rage as any Afrikaner. How does Trevelyan, then, fit into his theory that the English are good?

There is a debt he still owes Eddie, which he has told no one about. After he had bought the Smiths bicycle with the money for his eighth birthday and then found he did not know how to ride, it was Eddie who pushed him on Rosebank Common, shouting commands, till all of a sudden he mastered the art of balancing.

He rode in a wide loop that first time, pushing hard on the pedals to get through the sandy soil, till he came back to where Eddie was waiting. Eddie was excited, jumping up and down. '*Kan ek 'n kans kry?*' he clamoured—Can I have a turn? He passed the bicycle over to Eddie. Eddie didn't need to be pushed: he set off as fast as the wind, standing on the pedals, his old navy-blue blazer streaming behind him, riding a lot better than he did.

He remembers wrestling with Eddie on the lawn. Though Eddie was only seven months older than he, and no bigger, he had a wiry strength and a singleness of purpose that always made him the victor. The victor, but cautious in victory. Only for a moment, when he had his opponent pinned on his back, helpless, did Eddie allow himself a grin of triumph; then he rolled off and stood at a crouch, ready for the next round.

The smell of Eddie's body stays with him from these bouts, and the feel of his head, the high bullet-shaped skull and the close, coarse hair.

They have harder heads than white people, his father says. That is why they are so good at boxing. For the same reason, his father says, they will never be good at rugby. In rugby you have to think fast, you can't be a bonehead.

There is a moment as the two of them wrestle when his lips and nose are pressed against Eddie's hair. He breathes in the smell, the taste: the smell, the taste of smoke.

Every weekend Eddie had to give himself a bath, standing in a footbath in the servant's lavatory and washing himself with a soapy rag. He and his brother hauled a dustbin below the tiny window and climbed up to peek. Eddie was naked but for his leather belt, which he still wore around his waist. Seeing the two faces at the window, he gave a big smile and shouted *'Hê!'* and danced in the footbath, splashing the water, not covering himself.

Later he told his mother: 'Eddie didn't take off his belt in the bath.'

'Let him do what he wants,' said his mother.

He has never been to Ida's Valley, where Eddie comes from. He thinks of it as a cold, sodden place. In Eddie's mother's house there is no electric light. The roof leaks, everyone is always coughing. When you go outside you have to hop from stone to stone to avoid the puddles. What hope is there for Eddie now that he is back in Ida's Valley, in disgrace?

'What do you think Eddie is doing now?' he asks his mother.

'He is surely in a reformatory.'

'Why in a reformatory?'

'People like that always end up in a reformatory, and then in jail.'

He does not understand her bitterness against Eddie. He does not understand these bitter moods of hers, when things almost at random come under the disparaging lash of her tongue: Coloured people, her own brothers and sisters, books, education, the Government. He does not really care what she believes about Eddie as long as she does not change her mind from day to day. When she lashes out like this he feels that the floor is crumbling beneath his feet and he is falling.

He thinks of Eddie in his old blazer, crouching to hide from the rain that is always falling in Ida's Valley, smoking stompies with the older Coloured boys. He is ten and Eddie, in Ida's Valley, is ten. For a while Eddie will be eleven while he is still ten; then he will be eleven too. Always he will be pulling level, staying with Eddie for a while, then getting left behind. How long will it go on? Will he ever escape from Eddie? If they passed each other in the street one day, would Eddie, despite all his drinking and dagga-smoking, despite all the jail and all the hardening, recognize him and stop and shout '*Jou moer!*'

At this moment, in the leaky house in Ida's Valley, curled under a smelly blanket, still wearing his blazer, he knows that Eddie is thinking of him. In the dark Eddie's eyes are two yellow slits. One thing he knows for sure: Eddie will have no pity on him.

ELEVEN

OUTSIDE THEIR CIRCLE of kinfolk they have few social contacts.
On the occasions when strangers come to the house, he and his
brother scuttle away like wild animals, then sneak back to lurk
behind doors and eavesdrop. They have also pierced spy-holes
in the ceiling, so that they can climb into the roof-space and
peer into the living-room from above. Their mother is embarrassed by the scuffling noises. 'Just the children playing,' she
explains with a strained smile.

He flees polite talk because its formulas—'How are you?'
'How are you enjoying school?'—baffle him. Not knowing the
right answers, he mumbles and stammers like a fool. Yet finally
he is not ashamed of his wildness, his impatience with the tame
patter of genteel conversation.

'Can't you just be normal?' asks his mother.

'I hate normal people,' he replies hotly.

'I hate normal people,' his brother echoes. His brother is
seven. He wears a continual tight, nervous smile; at school he
sometimes throws up for no good reason and has to be fetched
home.

Instead of friends they have family. His mother's family are
the only people in the world who accept him more or less as he
is. They accept him—rude, unsocialized, eccentric—not only

because without accepting him they cannot come visiting, but because they too were brought up wild and rude. His father's family, on the other hand, disapprove of him and of the upbringing he has had at the hands of his mother. In their company he feels constrained; as soon as he can escape he begins to mock the commonplaces of politeness (*'En hoe gaan dit met jou mammie? En met jou broer? Dis goed, dis goed!'* How is your mommy? Your brother? Good!) Yet there is no evading them: without participating in their rituals there is no way of visiting the farm. So, squirming with embarrassment, despising himself for his cravenness, he submits. *'Dit gaan goed,'* he says. *'Dit gaan goed met ons almal.'* We're all fine.

He knows that his father sides with his family against him. This is one of his father's ways of getting back at his mother. He is chilled by the thought of the life he would face if his father ran the household, a life of dull, stupid formulas, of being like everyone else. His mother is the only one who stands between him and an existence he could not endure. So at the same time that he is irritated with her for her slowness and dullness, he clings to her as his only protector. He is her son, not his father's son. He denies and detests his father. He will not forget the day two years ago when his mother for the one and only time let his father loose on him, like a dog from a chain ('I've reached the limit, I can't stand it any more!'), and his father's eyes glared blue and angry as he shook him and cuffed him.

He must go to the farm because there is no place on earth he loves more or can imagine loving more. Everything that is complicated in his love for his mother is uncomplicated in his love for the farm. Yet since as far back as he can remember this love has had an edge of pain. He may visit the farm but he will never live there. The farm is not his home; he will never be more than a guest, an uneasy guest. Even now, day by day, the farm and he are travelling different roads, separating, growing not closer but further apart. One day the farm will be wholly gone, wholly lost; already he is grieving at that loss.

The farm used to be his grandfather's, but his grandfather died and it passed to Uncle Son, his father's elder brother. Son was the only one with an aptitude for farming; the rest of the brothers and sisters all too eagerly fled to the towns and cities. Nevertheless, there is a sense in which the farm on which they grew up is still theirs. So at least once a year, and sometimes twice, his father goes back to the farm and takes him along.

The farm is called Voëlfontein, Bird-fountain; he loves every stone of it, every bush, every blade of grass, loves the birds that give it its name, birds that as dusk falls gather in their thousands in the trees around the fountain, calling to each other, murmuring, ruffling their feathers, settling for the night. It is not conceivable that another person could love the farm as he does. But he cannot talk about his love, not only because normal people do not talk about such things but because confessing to it would be a betrayal of his mother. It would be a betrayal not only because she too comes from a farm, a rival farm in a far-off part of the world which she speaks of with a love and longing of her own but can never go back to because it was sold to strangers, but because she is not truly welcome on this farm, the real farm, Voëlfontein.

Why this is so she never explains—for which, in the end, he is grateful—but slowly he is able to piece the story together. For a long spell during the War, his mother lived with her two children in a single rented room in the town of Prince Albert, surviving on the six pounds a month his father remitted from his lance-corporal's pay plus two pounds from the Governor-General's Distress Fund. During this time they were not once invited to the farm, though the farm was a mere two hours away by road. He knows this part of the story because even his father, when he came back from the War, was angry and ashamed of how they had been treated.

Of Prince Albert he remembers only the whine of mosquitoes in the long hot nights, and his mother walking to and fro in her petticoat, sweat standing out on her skin, her heavy, fleshy legs crisscrossed with varicose veins, trying to soothe his baby brother, forever crying; and days of terrible boredom spent behind closed shutters sheltering from the sun. That was how they lived, stuck, too poor to move, waiting for the invitation that did not come.

His mother's lips still grow tight when the farm is mentioned. Nevertheless, when they go to the farm for Christmas she comes along. The whole extended family congregates. Beds and mattresses and stretchers are set out in every room, and on the long stoep too: one Christmas he counts twenty-six of them. All day long his aunt and the two maids are busy in the steamy kitchen, cooking, baking, producing meal after meal, one round of tea or coffee and cake after another, while the men sit on the stoep, gazing lazily over the shimmering Karoo, swapping stories about the old days.

Greedily he drinks in the atmosphere, drinks in the happy, slapdash mixture of English and Afrikaans that is their common tongue when they get together. He likes this funny, dancing language, with its particles that slip here and there in the sentence. It is lighter, airier than the Afrikaans they study at school, which is weighed down with idioms that are supposed to come from the *volksmond*, the people's mouth, but seem to come only from the Great Trek, lumpish, nonsensical idioms about wagons and cattle and cattle-harness.

On his first visit to the farm, while his grandfather was still alive, all the barnyard animals of his story-books were still

there: horses, donkeys, cows with their calves, pigs, ducks, a
colony of hens with a cock that crowed to greet the sun, nanny-
goats and bearded billy-goats. Then, after his grandfather's
death, the barnyard began to dwindle, till nothing was left but
sheep. First the horses were sold, then the pigs were turned into
pork (he watched his uncle shoot the last pig: the bullet took it
behind the ear: it gave a grunt and a great fart and collapsed,
first on its knees, then on its side, quivering). After that the cows
went, and the ducks.

The reason was the wool price. The Japanese were paying a
pound a pound for wool: it was easier to buy a tractor than keep
horses, easier to drive to Fraserburg Road in the new Studebaker and buy frozen butter and powdered milk than milk a cow
and churn the cream. Only sheep mattered, sheep with their
golden fleece.

The burden of agriculture could be shed too. The only crop
still grown on the farm is lucerne, in case the grazing runs out
and the sheep have to be fed. Of the orchards, only a grove of
orange-trees remains, yielding year after year the sweetest of
navels.

When, refreshed by an after-dinner nap, his aunts and
uncles congregate on the stoep to drink tea and tell stories, their
talk sometimes turns to old times on the farm. They reminisce
about their father the 'gentleman farmer' who kept a carriage
and pair, who grew corn on the lands below the dam which he
threshed and ground himself. 'Yes, those were the days,' they
say, and sigh.

They like to be nostalgic about the past, but none of them
want to go back to it. He does. He wants everything to be as it
was in the past.

In a corner of the stoep, in the shade of the bougainvillea,
hangs a canvas water-bottle. The hotter the day, the cooler the

water—a miracle, like the miracle of the meat that hangs in the dark of the storeroom and does not rot, like the miracle of the pumpkins that lie on the roof in the blazing sun and stay fresh. On the farm, it seems, there is no decay.

The water from the water-bottle is magically cool, but he pours no more than a mouthful at a time. He is proud of how little he drinks. It will stand him in good stead, he hopes, if he is ever lost in the veld. He wants to be a creature of the desert, this desert, like a lizard.

Just above the farmhouse is a stone-walled dam, twelve feet square, filled by a wind pump, which provides water for the house and garden. One hot day he and his brother launch a galvanized-iron bathtub into the dam, climb unsteadily in, and paddle it back and forth across the surface.

He fears water; he thinks of this adventure as a way of overcoming his fear. Their boat bobs about in the middle of the dam. Shafts of light flash from the dappled water; there is no sound but the trilling of cicadas. Between him and death there is only a thin sheet of metal. Nevertheless he feels quite secure, so secure that he can almost doze. This is the farm: no ill can happen here.

He has been in a boat only once before, when he was four. A man (who?—he tries to summon him up, but cannot) rowed them out on the lagoon at Plettenberg Bay. It was supposed to be a pleasure-trip, but all the while they rowed he sat frozen, fixing his eye on the far shore. Only once did he glance over the side. Fronds of water-grass rippled languidly deep below them. It was as he feared, and worse; his head spun. Only these fragile boards, which groaned with every oarstroke as if about to crack, kept him from plunging to his death. He gripped tighter and closed his eyes, beating down the panic inside him.

There are two Coloured families on Voëlfontein, each with a house of its own. There is also, near the dam wall, the house, now without a roof, in which Outa Jaap used to live. Outa Jaap was on the farm before his grandfather; he himself remembers Outa Jaap only as a very old man with milky-white, sightless eyeballs and toothless gums and knotted hands, sitting on a bench in the sun, to whom he was taken before he died, perhaps in order to be blessed, he is not sure. Though Outa Jaap is gone now, his name is still mentioned with deference. Yet when he asks what was special about Outa Jaap, the answers that come back are very ordinary. Outa Jaap came from the days before jackal-proof fences, he is told, when the shepherd who took his sheep to graze in one of the far-flung camps would be expected to live with them and guard them for weeks on end. Outa Jaap belonged to a vanished generation. That is all.

Nevertheless, he has a sense of what lies behind these words. Outa Jaap was part of the farm; though his grandfather may have been its purchaser and legal owner, Outa Jaap came with it, knew more about it, about sheep, veld, weather, than the new-comer would ever know. That was why Outa Jaap had to be de-ferred to; that is why there is no question of getting rid of Outa Jaap's son Ros, now in his middle years, though he is not a par-ticularly good workman, unreliable and prone to get things wrong.

It is understood that Ros will live and die on the farm and be succeeded by one of his sons. Freek, the other hired man, is younger and more energetic than Ros, quicker on the uptake and more dependable. Nevertheless, he is not of the farm: it is understood that he will not necessarily stay.

Coming to the farm from Worcester, where Coloured people seem to have to beg for whatever they get *(Asseblief my nooi! Asseblief my basie!),* he is relieved at how correct and formal rela-tions are between his uncle and the *volk.* Each morning his uncle confers with his two men about the day's tasks. He does

not give them orders. Instead he proposes the tasks that need to
be done, one by one, as if dealing cards on a table; his men deal
their own cards too. In between there are pauses, long, reflec-
tive silences in which nothing happens. Then all at once, mys-
teriously, the whole business seems to be settled: who will go
where, who will do what. *'Nouja, dan sal ons maar loop, baas
Sonnie!'*—We'll get going! And Ros and Freek don their hats
and briskly set off.

It is the same in the kitchen. There are two women who work
in the kitchen: Ros's wife Tryn, and Lientjie, his daughter from
another marriage. They arrive at breakfast-time and leave after
the midday meal, the main meal of the day, the meal that is here
called dinner. So shy is Lientjie of strangers that she hides her
face and giggles when spoken to. But if he stands at the kitchen
door he can hear, passing between his aunt and the two women,
a low stream of talk that he loves to eavesdrop on: the soft, comforting gossip of women, stories passed from ear to ear to ear, till
not only the farm but the village at Fraserburg Road and the location outside the village are covered by the stories, and all the
other farms of the district too: a soft white web of gossip spun
over past and present, a web being spun at the same moment
in other kitchens too, the Van Rensburg kitchen, the Alberts
kitchen, the Nigrini kitchen, the various Botes kitchens: who is
getting married to whom, whose mother-in-law is going to have
an operation for what, whose son is doing well at school, whose
daughter is in trouble, who visited whom, who wore what when.

But it is Ros and Freek with whom he has more to do. He
burns with curiosity about the lives they live. Do they wear vests
and underpants like white people? Do they each have a bed? Do
they sleep naked or in their work-clothes or do they have pyjamas? Do they eat proper meals, sitting at table with knives and
forks?

He has no way of answering these questions, for he is discouraged from visiting their houses. It would be rude, he is told—rude because Ros and Freek would find it embarrassing.

If it is not embarrassing to have Ros's wife and daughter work in the house, he wants to ask, cooking meals, washing clothes, making beds, why is it embarrassing to visit them in their house?

It sounds like a good argument, but there is a flaw in it, he knows. For the truth is that it *is* embarrassing to have Tryn and Lientjie in the house. He does not like it when he passes Lientjie in the passage and she has to pretend she is invisible and he has to pretend she is not there. He does not like to see Tryn on her knees at the washtub washing his clothes. He does not know how to answer her when she speaks to him in the third person, calling him '*die kleinbaas,*' the little master, as if he were not present. It is all deeply embarrassing.

It is easier with Ros and Freek. But even with them he has to speak tortuously constructed sentences to avoid calling them *jy* when they call him *kleinbaas*. He is not sure whether Freek counts as a man or a boy, whether he is making a fool of himself when he treats Freek as a man. With Coloured people in general, and with the people of the Karoo in particular, he simply does not know when they cease to be children and become men and women. It seems to happen so early and so suddenly: one day they are playing with toys, the next day they are out with the men, working, or in someone's kitchen, washing dishes.

Freek is gentle and soft-spoken. He has a bicycle with fat tyres and a guitar; in the evenings he sits outside his room and plays his guitar to himself, smiling his rather remote smile. On Saturday afternoons he cycles off to the Fraserburg Road location and stays there until Sunday evening, returning long after dark: from miles away they can see the tiny, wavering speck of light that is his bicycle lamp. It seems to him heroic to cycle that vast distance. He would hero-worship Freek if it were permitted.

Freek is a hired man, he is paid a wage, he can be given notice and sent packing. Nevertheless, seeing Freek sitting on his haunches, his pipe in his mouth, staring out over the veld, it seems to him that Freek belongs here more securely than the Coetzees do—if not to Voëlfontein, then to the Karoo. The Karoo is Freek's country, his home; the Coetzees, drinking tea and gossiping on the farmhouse stoep, are like swallows, seasonal, here today, gone tomorrow, or even like sparrows, chirping, light-footed, short-lived.

Best of all on the farm, best of everything, is the hunting. His uncle owns only one gun, a heavy Lee-Enfield .303 that fires a shell too large for any of the game (once his father shot a hare with it and nothing was left over but bloody scraps). So when he visits the farm they borrow from one of the neighbours an old .22. It takes a single cartridge, loaded straight into the breech; sometimes it misfires and he comes away with a singing in his ears that lasts for hours. He never manages to hit anything with this gun except frogs in the dam and muisvoëls in the orchard. Yet never does he lives more intensely than in the early mornings when he and his father set off with their guns up the dry bed of the Boesmansrivier in search of game: steenbok, duiker, hares, and, on the bare slopes of the hills, korhaan.

December after December he and his father come to the farm to hunt. They catch the train—not the Trans-Karoo Express or the Orange Express, to say nothing of the Blue Train, all of which are too expensive and anyhow do not stop at Fraserburg Road—but the ordinary passenger train, the one that stops at all the stations, even the most obscure, and sometimes has to creep into sidings and wait until the more famous expresses have flashed past. He loves this slow train, loves sleeping snug and tight under the crisp white sheets and navy-blue blankets that the bedding attendant brings, loves waking in the night at some quiet station in the middle of nowhere, hearing the hiss of the engine at rest, the clang of the ganger's hammer as he tests the wheels. And then at dawn, when they arrive at Fraserburg Road, Uncle Son will be waiting for them, wearing his broad smile and his old, oil-stained felt hat, saying '*Jis-laaik, maar jy word darem groot, John!*'—You're getting big!—and whistling through his teeth, and they can load their bags on the Studebaker and set off on the long drive.

He accepts without question the variety of hunting practised on Voëlfontein. He accepts that they have had a good hunt if they start a single hare or hear a pair of korhaan gargling in the distance. That is enough of a story to tell the rest of the family, who, by the time they return with the sun high in the sky, are sitting on the stoep drinking coffee. Most mornings they have nothing to report, nothing at all.

There is no point in going out to hunt in the heat of the day, when the animals they want to slay are dozing in the shade. But in the late afternoon they sometimes go touring the farm roads in the Studebaker, with Uncle Son driving and his father in the passenger seat holding the .303 and he and Ros in the dickey seat at the back.

Normally it would be Ros's job to jump out and open the camp gates for the car, wait for the car to go through, and then close the gates behind, one gate after another. But on these hunts it is his privilege to open the gates, while Ros watches and approves.

They are hunting the fabled paauw. However, since paauw are sighted only once or twice a year—so rare are they, indeed, that there is a fine of fifty pounds for shooting them, if you are caught—they settle for hunting korhaan. Ros is taken along on the hunt because, being a Bushman or nearly a Bushman, he must have preternaturally sharp vision.

And indeed it is Ros, with a slap on the roof of the car, who sees the korhaan first: grey-brown birds the size of pullets trotting among the bushes in groups of two or three. The Studebaker comes to a halt; his father rests the .303 on the window and takes aim; the clap of the shot echoes back and forth across the veld. Sometimes the birds, alarmed, take flight; more often they simply trot faster, making their characteristic gargling noise. Never does his father actually hit a korhaan, so never does he get to see one of these birds ('bush-bustard,' says the Afrikaans-English dictionary) from close by.

His father was a gunner in the war: he manned a Bofors anti-aircraft gun shooting at German and Italian planes. He wonders whether he ever shot a plane down: he certainly never boasts of it. How did he come to be a gunner at all? He has no gift for it. Were soldiers just allotted things to do at random?

The only variety of hunting at which they do succeed is hunting by night, which, he soon discovers, is shameful and not to be boasted about. The method is simple. After supper they climb aboard the Studebaker and Uncle Son drives them in darkness across the lucerne fields. At a certain point he stops and switches on the headlights. Not thirty yards away a steenbok stands frozen, its ears cocked toward them, its dazzled eyes reflecting the lights. '*Skiet!*' hisses his uncle. His father shoots and the buck falls.

They tell themselves it is acceptable to hunt in this way because the buck are a pest, eating lucerne that should go to the sheep. But when he sees how tiny the dead buck is, no larger than a poodle, he knows the argument is hollow. They hunt by night because they are not good enough to shoot anything by day.

On the other hand, the venison, steeped in vinegar and then roasted (he watches his aunt cut slits in the dark flesh and stuff it with cloves and garlic), is even more delicious than lamb, tangy and soft, so soft that it melts in the mouth. Everything in the Karoo is delicious, the peaches, the watermelons, the pumpkin, the mutton, as though whatever can find sustenance in this arid earth is thereby blessed.

They will never be famous hunters. Still, he loves the heft of the gun in his hand, the sound of their feet tramping the grey river-sand, the silence that descends heavy as a cloud when they stop, and always the landscape enclosing them, the beloved landscape of ochre and grey and fawn and olive-green.

On the last day of the visit, according to ritual, he may shoot up the remainder of his box of .22 cartridges at a tin can on a fence-post. It is a difficult occasion. The borrowed gun is not a good one, he is not a good shot. With the family watching from the stoep, he fires off his shots hastily, missing more often than he hits.

One morning while he is out by himself in the river-bed, hunting muisvoëls, the .22 jams. He cannot find a way to release the cartridge-case stuck in the breech. He brings the gun back to the house, but Uncle Son and his father are away in the veld. 'Ask Ros or Freek,' his mother suggests. He seeks out Freek in the stable. Freek, however, does not want to touch the gun. It is the same with Ros, when he finds Ros. Though they will not explain themselves, they seem to have a holy terror of guns. So he has to wait for his uncle to come back and prise out the cartridge-case with his penknife. 'I asked Ros and Freek,' he complains, 'but they wouldn't help.' His uncle shakes his head. 'You mustn't ask them to touch guns,' he says. 'They know they mustn't.'

They mustn't. Why not? No one will tell him. But he broods

on the word *mustn't*. He hears it more often on the farm than anywhere else, more often even than in Worcester. A strange word, easy to misspell because of the silent *t* hidden in the middle. 'You mustn't touch this.' 'You mustn't eat that.' Would that be the price, if he were to give up going to school and plead to live here on the farm: that he would have to stop asking questions, obey all the *mustn't*s, just do as he was told? Would he be prepared to knuckle down and pay that price? Is there no way of living in the Karoo—the only place in the world where he wants to be—as he wants to live: without belonging to a family?

The farm is huge, so huge that when, on one of their hunts, he and his father come to a fence across the river-bed, and his father announces that they have reached the boundary between Voëlfontein and the next farm, he is taken aback. In his imagination Voëlfontein is a kingdom in its own right. There is not enough time in a single life to know all of Voëlfontein, know its every stone and bush. No time can be enough when one loves a place with such devouring love.

He knows Voëlfontein best in summer, when it lies flattened under an even, blinding light that pours down from the sky. Yet Voëlfontein has its mysteries too, mysteries that belong not to night and shadow but to hot afternoons when mirages dance on the horizon and the very air sings in his ears. Then, when everyone else is dozing, stunned by the heat, he can tiptoe out of the house and climb the hill to the labyrinth of stone-walled kraals that belong to the old days when the sheep in their thousands had to be brought in from the veld to be counted or shorn or dipped. The kraal walls are two feet thick and higher than his head; they are made of flat blue-grey stones, every one of them trundled here by donkey-cart. He tries to picture the herds of sheep, all of them dead and gone now, that must have sheltered from the sun in the lee of these walls. He tries to picture Voëlfontein as it must have been when the great house and its out-buildings and kraals were still in the process of being built: a site of patient, ant-like labour, year after year. Now the jackals that preyed on the sheep have been exterminated, shot or poisoned, and the kraals, without a use, are sliding into ruin.

The kraal walls ramble for miles up and down the hillside. Nothing grows here: the earth has been trampled flat and killed forever, he does not know how: it has a stained, unhealthy, yellow look. Once inside the walls, he is cut off from everything save the sky. He has been warned not to come here because of the danger of snakes, because no one will hear him if he shouts for help. Snakes, he is warned, revel in hot afternoons like these: they come out of their lairs—ringhals, puff-adder, skaap-steker—to bask in the sun, warming their cold blood.

He has yet to see a snake in the kraals; nevertheless, he watches his every step.

Freek comes across a skaapsteker behind the kitchen, where the women hang the laundry. He beats it to death with a stick and drapes the long, yellow body over a bush. For weeks the women will not go there. Snakes marry for life, says Tryn; when you kill the male, the female comes in search of revenge.

Spring, September, is the best time to visit the Karoo, though the school vacation is only one week long. They are on the farm one September when the shearers arrive. They appear from no-where, wild men who come on bicycles laden with bedrolls and pots and pans.

Shearers, he discovers, are special people. When they descend on the farm, it is good luck. To hold them there, a fat *hamel*, a wether, is picked out and slaughtered. They take possession of the old stable, which they turn into their barracks. A fire burns late into the night as they feast.

He listens to a long discussion between Uncle Son and their

leader, a man so dark and fierce he could almost be a Native, with a pointed beard and trousers held up by rope. They talk about the weather, about the state of the grazing in the Prince Albert district, in the Beaufort district, in the Fraserburg district, about payment. The Afrikaans the shearers speak is so thick, so full of strange idioms, that he can barely understand it. Where do they come from? Is there a country deeper even than the country of Voëlfontein, a heartland even more secluded from the world?

The next morning, an hour before dawn, he is woken by the trampling of hooves as the first troops of sheep are driven past the house to be penned in the kraals beside the shearing-shed. The household begins to awake. There is a bustle in the kitchen, and the smell of coffee. By first light he is outside, dressed, too excited to eat.

He is given a task. He has charge of a tin mug full of dried beans. Each time a shearer finishes a sheep, and releases it with a slap on the hindquarters, and tosses the shorn pelt on to the sorting-table, and the sheep, pink and naked and bleeding where the shears have nipped it, trots nervously into the second pen—each time, the shearer may take a bean from the mug, which he does with a nod and a courteous 'My basie!'

When he is tired of holding the mug (the shearers can take the beans for themselves, they are country-bred and have never so much as heard of dishonesty), he and his brother help with the stuffing of the bales, jumping up and down on the mass of thick, hot, oily wool. His cousin Agnes is there too, visiting from Skipperskloof. She and her sister join in; the four of them tumble over each other, giggling and cavorting as if in a huge featherbed.

Agnes occupies a place in his life that he does not yet understand. He first set eyes on her when he was seven. Invited to

Skipperskloof, they arrived late one afternoon after a long train journey. Clouds scudded across the sky, there was no warmth in the sun. Under the chill winter light the veld stretched out a deep reddish blue without trace of green. Even the farmhouse looked unwelcoming: an austere white rectangle with a steep zinc roof. It was not at all like Voëlfontein; he did not want to be there.

Agnes, a few months older than himself, was allotted to be his companion. She took him for a walk in the veld. She went barefoot; she did not even own shoes. Soon they were out of sight of the house, in the middle of nowhere. They began to talk. She had pigtails and a lisp, which he liked. He lost his reserve. As he spoke he forgot what language he was speaking: thoughts simply turned to words within him, transparent words.

What he said to Agnes that afternoon he can no longer remember. But he told her everything, everything he did, everything he knew, everything he hoped for. In silence she took it all in. Even as he spoke he knew the day was special because of her.

The sun began to sink, fiery crimson yet icy. The clouds darkened, the wind grew sharper, cutting through his clothes. Agnes was wearing nothing but a thin cotton dress; her feet were blue with cold.

'Where have you been? What have you been doing?' asked the grown-ups when they returned to the house. '*Niks nie,*' answered Agnes. Nothing.

Here on Voëlfontein Agnes is not allowed to go hunting, but she is free to wander with him in the veld or catch frogs with him in the big earth-dam. Being with her is different from being with his school friends. It has something to do with her softness, her readiness to listen, but also with her slim brown legs, her bare feet, the way she dances from stone to stone. He is clever, he is top of his class; she is reputed to be clever too; they roam around talking about things that the grown-ups would shake their heads over: whether the universe had a beginning; what lies beyond Pluto, the dark planet; where God is, if he exists.

Why is it that he can speak so easily to Agnes? Is it because she is a girl? To whatever comes from him she seems to answer without reserve, softly, readily. She is his first cousin, therefore they cannot fall in love and get married. In a way that is a relief: he is free to be friends with her, open his heart to her. But is he in love with her nevertheless? Is this love—this easy generosity, this sense of being understood at last, of not having to pretend?

All day and all of the next day the shearers work, barely stopping to eat, calling out challenges to each other to prove who is fastest. By evening on the second day all the work is done, every sheep on the farm has been shorn. Uncle Son brings out a canvas bag full of notes and coins, and each shearer is paid according to his number of beans. Then there is another fire, another feast. The next morning they are gone and the farm can return to its old, slow ways.

The bales of wool are so many that they overflow the shed. Uncle Son goes from one to another with a stencil and ink-pad, painting on each his name, the name of the farm, the grade of wool. Days later a huge lorry arrives (how did it get across the sand-bed of the Boesmansrivier, where even cars stall?) and the bales are loaded and driven away.

Every year this happens. Every year the shearers come, every year there is this adventure and excitement. It will never end; there is no reason why it should ever end, as long as there are years.

The secret and sacred word that binds him to the farm is *belong*. Out in the veld by himself he can breathe the word aloud: *I belong on the farm*. What he really believes but does not utter, what he keeps to himself for fear that the spell will end, is a different form of the word: *I belong to the farm.*

He tells no one because the word is misunderstood so easily, turned so easily into its inverse: *The farm belongs to me.* The farm will never belong to him, he will never be more than a visitor: he accepts that. The thought of actually living on Voëlfontein, of calling the great old house his home, of no longer having to ask permission to do what he wants to do, turns him giddy; he thrusts it away. *I belong to the farm:* that is the furthest he is prepared to go, even in his most secret heart. But in his secret heart he knows what the farm in its way knows too: that Voëlfontein belongs to no one. The farm is greater than any of them. The farm exists from eternity to eternity. When they are all dead, when even the farmhouse has fallen into ruin like the kraals on the hillside, the farm will still be here.

Once, out in the veld far from the house, he bends down and rubs his palms in the dust as if washing them. It is ritual. He is making up a ritual. He does not know yet what the ritual means, but he is relieved there is no one to see and report him.

Belonging to the farm is his secret fate, a fate he was born into but embraces gladly. His other secret is that, fight though he may, he still belongs to his mother. It does not escape him that these two servitudes clash. Nor does it escape him that on the farm his mother's hold is at its weakest. Unable, as a woman, to hunt, unable even to walk about in the veld, she is here at a disadvantage.

He has two mothers. Twice-born: born from woman and born from the farm. Two mothers and no father.

Half a mile from the farmhouse the road breaks in two, the left fork going to Merweville, the right to Fraserburg. At the fork is the graveyard, a fenced plot with a gate of its own. Dominating the graveyard is his grandfather's marble headstone; clustered around it are a dozen other graves, lower and simpler, with headstones of slate, some with names and dates chipped into them, some with no words at all.

His grandfather is the only Coetzee there, the only one who has died since the farm passed into the family. This is where he ended, the man who began as a pedlar in Piketberg, then opened a shop in Laingsburg and became mayor of the town, then bought the hotel at Fraserburg Road. He lies buried, but the farm is still his. His children run like midgets on it, and his grandchildren, midgets of midgets.

On the other side of the road is a second graveyard, without a fence, where some of the grave-mounds are so weathered that they have been reabsorbed into the earth. Here lie the servants and hirelings of the farm, stretching back to Outa Jaap and far beyond. What few gravestones still stand are without names or dates. Yet here he feels more awe than among the generations of Botes clustering around his grandfather. It has nothing to do with spirits. No one in the Karoo believes in spirits. Whatever dies here dies firmly and finally: its flesh is picked off by the ants, its bones are bleached by the sun, and that is that. Yet among these graves he treads nervously. From the earth comes a deep silence, so deep that it could almost be a hum.

When he dies he wants to be buried on the farm. If they will not permit that, then he wants to be cremated and have his ashes scattered here.

The other place to which he does pilgrimage each year is Bloemhof, where the first farmhouse stood. Nothing remains now but the foundations, which are of no interest. In front of it there used to be a dam fed by an underground fountain; but the fountain long ago dried up. Of the garden and orchard that once grew here there is no trace. But beside the fountain, growing out of the bare earth, stands a huge, lonely palm-tree. In the stem of this tree bees have made a nest, fierce little black bees. The trunk is blackened with the smoke of fires that people have lit over the years in order to rob the bees of their honey; yet the bees stay on, gathering nectar who knows where in this dry, grey landscape.

He would like the bees to recognize that he, when he visits, comes with clean hands, not to steal from them but to greet them, to pay his respects. But as he nears the palm-tree they begin to buzz angrily; outriders swoop upon him, warning him away; once he has even to flee, running ignominiously across the veld with the swarm behind him, zigzagging and waving his arms, thankful there is no one to see him and laugh.

Every Friday a sheep is slaughtered for the people of the farm. He goes along with Ros and Uncle Son to pick out the one that is to die; then he stands by and watches as, in the slaughtering-place behind the shed, out of sight of the house, Freek holds down the legs while Ros, with his harmless-looking little pocket-knife, cuts its throat, and then both men hold tight as the animal kicks and struggles and coughs while its lifeblood gushes out. He continues to watch as Ros flays the still warm body and hangs the carcase from the seringa tree and splits it open and tugs the insides out into a basin: the great blue stomach full of grass, the intestines (from the bowel he squeezes out the last few droppings that the sheep did not have time to drop), the heart, the liver, the kidneys—all the things that a sheep has inside it and that he has inside him too.

Ros uses the same knife to castrate lambs. That event he watches too. The young lambs and their mothers are rounded up and penned. Then Ros moves among them, snatching lambs by the hind leg, one by one, pressing them to the ground while they bleat in terror, one despairing wail after another, and slitting open the scrotum. His head bobs down, he catches the testicles in his teeth and tugs them out. They look like two little jellyfish trailing blue and red blood-vessels.

Ros slices off the tail as well, while he is about it, and tosses it aside, leaving a bloody stump.

With his short legs, his baggy, castoff pants cut off below the knees, his homemade shoes and tattered felt hat, Ros shuffles about the pen like a clown, picking out the lambs, doctoring them pitilessly. At the end of the operation the lambs stand sore and bleeding by their mothers' side, who have done nothing to protect them. Ros folds his pocket-knife. The job is done; he wears a tight little smile.

There is no way of talking about what he has seen. 'Why do they have to cut off the lambs' tails?' he asks his mother. 'Because otherwise the blowflies would breed under their tails,' his mother replies. They are both pretending; both of them know what the question is really about.

Once Ros lets him hold his pocket-knife, shows him how easily it cuts a hair. The hair does not bend, just springs in two at the merest touch of the blade. Ros sharpens the knife every day, spitting on the whetstone, brushing the blade across it back and forth, lightly, easily. So much of the blade has been worn away with all the sharpening and all the cutting and all the sharpening again that there is only a sliver left. It is the same with Ros's spade: so long has he used it, so often sharpened it, that only an inch or two of steel remains; the wood of the grip is smooth and black with years of sweat.

'You shouldn't be watching that,' says his mother, after one of the Friday slaughterings.

'Why?'

'You just shouldn't.'

'I want to.'

And he goes off to watch Ros peg down the skin and sprinkle it with rock-salt.

He likes watching Ros and Freek and his uncle at work. To take advantage of the high wool prices, Son wants to run more sheep on the farm. But after years of poor rain the veld is a desert, grass and bushes cropped to the ground. He therefore sets about re-fencing the entire farm, breaking it into smaller camps so that the sheep can be shifted from camp to camp and the veld given time to recover. He and Ros and Freek go out every day, driving fence-posts into the rock-hard earth, spanning furlong after furlong of wire, drawing it taut as a bowstring, clamping it.

Uncle Son always treats him kindly, yet he knows he does not really like him. How does he know? By the uneasy look in Son's eyes when he is around, the forced tone in his voice. If Son really liked him, he would be as free and offhand with him as he is with Ros and Freek. Instead, Son is careful always to speak English to him, even though he speaks Afrikaans back. It has become a point of honour with both of them; they do not know how to get out of the trap.

He tells himself that the dislike is not personal, that it is only because he, the son of Son's younger brother, is older than Son's own son, who is still a baby. But he fears that the feeling runs deeper, that Son disapproves of him because he has given his allegiance to his mother, the interloper, rather than to his father; also because he is not straight, honest, truthful.

If he had a choice between Son and his own father as a father, he would choose Son, even though that would mean he would be irrecoverably Afrikaans and would have to spend years in the purgatory of an Afrikaans boarding-school, as all farm-children do, before he would be allowed to come back to the farm.

Perhaps that is the deeper reason why Son dislikes him: he feels the obscure claim this strange child is making on him and rejects it, like a man shaking himself free of a clinging baby.

He watches Son all the time, admiring the skill with which he does everything from dosing a sick animal to repairing a wind-pump. He is particularly fascinated by his knowledge of sheep. By looking at a sheep, Son can tell not only its age and its parentage, not only what kind of wool it will give, but what each part of its body will taste like. He can pick out a slaughter-sheep according to whether it has the right ribs for grilling or the right haunches for roasting.

He himself likes meat. He looks forward to the tinkle of the bell at midday and the huge repast it announces: dishes of roast potatoes, yellow rice with raisins, sweet potatoes with caramel sauce, pumpkin with brown sugar and soft bread-cubes, sweet-and-sour beans, beetroot salad, and, at the centre, in pride of place, a great platter of mutton with gravy to pour over it. Yet after seeing Ros slaughtering sheep he no longer likes to handle raw meat. Back in Worcester he prefers not to go into butchers' shops. He is repelled by the casual ease with which the butcher slaps down a cut of meat on the counter, slices it, rolls it up in brown paper, writes a price on it. When he hears the grating whine of the bandsaw cutting through bone, he wants to stop his ears. He does not mind looking at livers, whose function in the body is vague, but he turns his eyes away from the hearts in the display case, and particularly from the trays of offal. Even on the farm he refuses to eat offal, though it is considered a great delicacy.

He does not understand why sheep accept their fate, why they never rebel but instead go meekly to their death. If buck know that there is nothing worse on earth than falling into the hands of men, and to their last breath struggle to escape, why are sheep so stupid? They are animals, after all, they have the sharp senses of animals: why do they not hear the last bleatings of the victim behind the shed, smell its blood, and take note?

Sometimes when he is among the sheep—when they have been rounded up to be dipped, and are penned tight and cannot get away—he wants to whisper to them, warn them of what lies in store. But then in their yellow eyes he catches a glimpse of something that silences him: a resignation, a foreknowledge not only of what happens to sheep at the hands of Ros behind the shed, but of what awaits them at the end of the long, thirsty ride to Cape Town on the transport lorry. They know it all, down to the finest detail, and yet they submit. They have calculated the price and are prepared to pay it—the price of being on earth, the price of being alive.

TWELVE

IN WORCESTER the wind is always blowing, thin and cold in the winter, hot and dry in summer. After an hour outdoors there is a fine red dust in one's hair, in one's ears, on one's tongue.

He is healthy, full of life and energy, yet seems always to have a cold. In the mornings he wakes up tight-throated, red-eyed, sneezing uncontrollably, his body-temperature soaring and plunging. 'I'm sick,' he croaks to his mother. She rests the back of her hand against his forehead. 'Then you must surely stay in bed,' she sighs.

There is one more difficult moment to get through, the moment when his father says, 'Where's John?' and his mother says, 'He's sick,' and his father snorts and says, 'Pretending again.' Through this he lies as quiet as he can, till his father is gone and his brother is gone and he can at last settle down to a day of reading.

He reads at great speed and with total absorption. During his sick spells his mother has to visit the library twice a week to take out books for him: two on her cards, another two on his own. He avoids the library himself in case the librarian asks questions when he brings his books to be stamped.

He knows that if he wants to be a great man he ought to be reading serious books. He ought to be like Abraham Lincoln or James Watt, studying by candlelight while everyone else is sleeping, teaching himself Latin and Greek and astronomy. He has not abandoned the idea of being a great man; he promises himself he will soon begin serious reading; but for the present all he wants to read are stories.

He reads all the Enid Blyton mystery stories, all the Hardy Boys stories, all the Biggles stories. But the books he likes best are the French Foreign Legion stories of P C Wren. 'Who is the greatest writer in the world?' he asks his father. His father says Shakespeare. 'Why not P C Wren?' he says. His father has not read P C Wren and, despite his soldiering background, does not seem interested in doing so. 'P C Wren wrote forty-six books. How many books did Shakespeare write?' he challenges, and starts reciting titles. His father says 'Aah!' in an irritated, dismissive way but has no reply.

If his father likes Shakespeare then Shakespeare must be bad, he decides. Nevertheless, he begins to read Shakespeare, in the yellowing edition with the tattered edges that his father inherited and that may be worth lots of money because it is old, trying to discover why people say Shakespeare is great. He reads *Titus Andronicus* because of its Roman name, then *Coriolanus*, skipping the long speeches as he skips the nature descriptions in his library books.

Besides Shakespeare, his father owns the poems of Wordsworth and the poems of Keats. His mother owns the poems of Rupert Brooke. These poetry books have pride of place on the mantelshelf in the living-room, along with Shakespeare, *The Story of San Michele* in a leather slip-case, and a book by A J Cronin about a doctor. Twice he tries to read *The Story of San Michele*, but gets bored. He can never work out who Axel Munthe is, whether the book is true or a story, whether it is about a girl or a place.

One day his father comes to his room with the Wordsworth book. 'You should read these,' he says, and points out poems he has ticked in pencil. A few days later he comes back, wanting to discuss the poems. 'The sounding cataract haunted me like a passion,' his father quotes. 'It's great poetry, isn't it?' He mumbles, refuses to meet his father's eye, refuses to play the game. It is not long before his father gives up.

He is not sorry about his churlishness. He cannot see how poetry fits into his father's life; he suspects it is just pretence. When his mother says that in order to escape the mockery of her sisters she had to take her book and creep away in the loft, he believes her. But he cannot imagine his father, as a boy, reading poetry, who nowadays reads nothing but the newspaper. All he can imagine his father doing at that age is joking and laughing and smoking cigarettes behind the bushes.

He watches his father reading the newspaper. He reads quickly, nervously, flipping through the pages as though looking for something that is not there, cracking and slapping the pages as he turns them. When he is done with reading he folds the paper into a narrow panel and does the crossword puzzle.

His mother too reveres Shakespeare. She thinks *Macbeth* is Shakespeare's greatest play. 'If but the something could trammel up the consequences then it were,' she gabbles, and comes to a stop; 'and bring with his surcease success,' she continues, nodding to keep the beat. 'All the perfumes of Arabia could not wash this little hand,' she adds. *Macbeth* was the play she studied in school; her teacher used to stand behind her, pinching her arm until she had recited the whole of the speech. *'Kom nou, Vera!'* he used to say—'Come on!'—pinching her, and she would bring out a few more words.

What he cannot understand about his mother is that, though she is so stupid that she cannot help him with his Standard Four homework, her English is faultless, particularly when she writes. She uses words in their right sense, her grammar is impeccable. She is at home in the language, it is an area where she cannot be shaken. How did it happen? Her father was Piet Wehmeyer, a flat Afrikaans name. In the photograph album, in his collarless shirt and wide-brimmed hat, he looks like any ordinary farmer. In the Uniondale district where they lived there were no English; all the neighbours seem to have been named Zondagh. Her own mother was born Marie du Biel, of German parents with not a drop of English blood in their veins. Yet when she had children she gave them English names—Roland, Winifred, Ellen, Vera, Norman, Lancelot—and spoke English to them at home. Where could they have learned English, she and Piet?

His father's English is nearly as good, though his accent has more than a trace of Afrikaans in it and he says 'thutty' for 'thirty.' His father is always turning the pages of the Pocket Oxford English Dictionary for his crossword puzzles. He seems at least distantly familiar with every word in the dictionary, and every idiom too. He pronounces the more nonsensical idioms with relish, as though consolidating them in his memory: *pitch in, come a cropper.*

He himself does not read further than *Coriolanus* in the Shakespeare book. But for the sports page and the comic strips, the newspaper bores him. When he has nothing else to read, he reads the green books. 'Bring me a green book!' he calls to his mother from his sick-bed. The green books are Arthur Mee's *Children's Encyclopaedia*, which have been travelling with them ever since he can remember. He has been through them scores of times; when he was still a baby he tore pages out of them, scrawled over them with crayons, broke their bindings, so that now they have to be handled gingerly.

He does not actually read the green books: the prose makes

him too impatient, it is too gushing and childish, except for the second half of volume 10, the index, which is full of factual information. But he pores over the pictures, particularly the photographs of marble sculptures, naked men and women with wisps of cloth around their middles. Smooth, slim marble girls fill his erotic dreams.

The surprising thing about his colds is how quickly they clear up or seem to clear up. By eleven in the morning the sneezing has stopped, the stuffiness in his head has lifted, he feels fine. He has had enough of his sweaty, smelly pyjamas, of the stale blankets and sagging mattress, the soggy handkerchiefs all over the place. He gets out of bed but does not get dressed: that would be pressing his luck too far. Cautious not to show his face outdoors in case a neighbour or passer-by reports him, he plays with his Meccano set or sticks stamps in his album or threads buttons on strings or braids cords out of leftover skeins of wool. His drawer is full of cords he has braided, that have no use except as belts for the dressing-gown he does not have. When his mother comes into his room he looks as hangdog as he can, bracing himself against her caustic remarks.

On every side he is suspected of being a cheat. He can never persuade his mother that he is really sick; when she gives in to his pleas, she does so ungraciously, and only because she does not know how to say no to him. His schoolfellows think he is a namby-pamby and a mother's darling.

Yet the truth is that many mornings he wakes struggling for breath; bouts of sneezing convulse him for minutes on end, till he is panting and weeping and wants to die. There is no feigning in these colds of his.

The rule is that when you have been absent from school, you have to bring a letter of excuse. He knows his mother's standard letter by heart: 'Please excuse John's absence yesterday. He was suffering from a bad cold, and I thought it advisable for him to stay in bed. Yours faithfully.' He hands in these letters, which his mother writes as lies and which are read as lies, with an apprehensive heart.

When at the end of the year he counts the days he has missed, they come to almost one in three. Yet he still comes first in class. The conclusion he draws is that what goes on in the classroom is of no importance. He can always catch up at home. If he had his way, he would stay away from school all year, making an appearance only to write the examinations.

Nothing his teachers say is not already written in the textbook. He does not look down on them for that, nor do the other boys. In fact he does not like it when, now and then, a teacher's ignorance is exposed. He would protect his teachers if he could. He listens with attention to their every word. But he listens less in order to learn than in case he is caught daydreaming ('What did I just say? Repeat what I just said'), in case he is called out in front of the class and humiliated.

He is convinced that he is different, special. What he does not yet know is why he is in the world. He suspects he will not be an Arthur or an Alexander, revered in his lifetime. Not until after he is dead will he be appreciated.

He is waiting to be called. When the call comes, he will be ready. Unflinchingly he will answer, even if it means going to his death, like the men of the Light Brigade.

The standard he subjects himself to is the standard of the VC, the Victoria Cross. Only the English have the VC. The Americans do not have it, nor, to his disappointment, do the Russians. The South Africans certainly do not have it.

He does not fail to notice that VC are his mother's initials.

South Africa is a country without heroes. Wolraad Woltemade would perhaps count as a hero if he did not have such a funny name. Swimming out into the stormy sea time and time again to save hapless sailors is certainly courageous; but did the courage belong to the man or to the horse? The thought of Wolraad Woltemade's white horse steadfastly plunging back into the waves (he loves the redoubled, steady force of *steadfast*) brings a lump to his throat.

Vic Toweel fights against Manuel Ortiz for the bantamweight title of the world. The fight takes place on a Saturday night; he stays up late with his father to listen to the commentary on the radio. In the last round Toweel, bleeding and exhausted, hurls himself at his opponent. Ortiz reels; the crowd goes wild, the commentator's voice is hoarse with shouting. The judges announce their decision: South Africa's Viccie Toweel is the new champion of the world. He and his father shout with elation and embrace each other. He does not know how to express his joy. Impulsively he grips his father's hair, tugs with all his might. His father starts back, looks at him oddly.

For days the newspapers are full of pictures of the fight. Viccie Toweel is a national hero. As for him, his elation soon dwindles. He is still happy that Toweel has beaten Ortiz, but has begun to wonder why. Who is Toweel to him? Why should he not be free to choose between Toweel and Ortiz in boxing as he is free to choose between Hamiltons and Villagers in rugby? Is he bound to support Toweel, this ugly little man with hunched shoulders and a big nose and tiny blank, black eyes, because Toweel (despite his funny name) is a South African? Do South Africans have to support other South Africans even if they don't know them?

His father is no help. His father never says anything surprising. Unfailingly he predicts that South Africa is going to win or that Western Province is going to win, whether at rugby or cricket or anything else. 'Who do you think is going to win?' he challenges his father the day before Western Province plays Transvaal. 'Western Province, by a mile,' responds his father like clockwork. They listen to the match on the radio and Transvaal wins. His father is unshaken. 'Next year Western Province will win,' he says: 'just watch.'

It seems to him stupid to believe that Western Province will win just because you come from Cape Town. Better to believe that Transvaal will win, and then get a nice surprise if they don't.

In his hand he retains the feel of his father's hair, coarse, sturdy. The violence of his action still puzzles and disturbs him. He has never been so free with his father's body before. He would prefer that it did not happen again.

THIRTEEN

IT IS LATE AT NIGHT. Everyone else is asleep. He is lying in bed, remembering. Across his bed falls a strip of orange from the street-lights that burn all night over Reunion Park.

He is remembering what happened that morning during assembly, while the Christians were singing their hymns and the Jews and Catholics were roaming free. Two older boys, Catholics, had penned him in a corner. 'When are you coming to catechism?' they had demanded. 'I can't come to catechism, I have to do errands for my mother on Friday afternoons,' he had lied. 'If you don't come to catechism you can't be a Catholic,' they had said. 'I am a Catholic,' he had insisted, lying again.

If the worst were to happen, he thinks now, facing the worst, if the Catholic priest were to visit his mother and ask why he never comes to catechism, or—the other nightmare—if the school principal were to announce that all boys with Afrikaans names were to be transferred to Afrikaans classes—if nightmare were to turn to reality and he were left with no recourse but to retreat into petulant shouting and storming and crying, into the baby behaviour that he knows is still inside him, coiled like a spring—if, after that tempest, he were as a last, desperate step to throw himself upon his mother's protection, refusing to go back to school, pleading with her to save him—if he were in this way to disgrace himself utterly and finally, revealing what only he in his way and his mother in her way and perhaps his father in his own scornful way know, namely that he is still a baby and will never grow up—if all the stories that have been built up around him, built by himself, built by years of normal behaviour, at least in public, were to collapse, and the ugly, black, crying, babyish core of him were to emerge for all to see and laugh at, would there be any way in which he could go on living? Would he not have become as bad as one of those deformed, stunted, mongol children with hoarse voices and slavering lips that might as well be given sleeping pills or strangled?

All the beds in the house are old and tired, their springs sag, they creak at the slightest movement. He lies as still as he can in the sliver of light from the window, conscious of his body drawn up on its side, of his fists clenched against his chest. In this silence he tries to imagine his death. He subtracts himself from everything: from the school, from the house, from his mother; he tries to imagine the days wheeling through their course without him. But he cannot. Always there is something left behind, something small and black, like a nut, like an acorn that has been in the fire, dry, ashy, hard, incapable of growth, but *there*. He can imagine himself dying but he cannot imagine himself disappearing. Try as he will, he cannot annihilate the last residue of himself.

What is it that keeps him in existence? Is it fear of his mother's grief, grief so great that he cannot bear to think of it for more than a flash? (He sees her in a bare room, standing silent, her hands covering her eyes; then he draws the blind on her, on the image.) Or is there something else in him that refuses to die?

He remembers the other time he was cornered, when the two Afrikaans boys pinned his hands behind his back and marched him behind the earth-wall at the far end of the rugby field. He remembers the bigger boy in particular, so fat that the fat flowed over his tight clothes——one of those idiots or near-idiots who can break your fingers or crush your windpipe as easily as they wring a bird's neck and smile placidly while they are doing it. He had been afraid, there was no doubt of that, his heart had been hammering. Yet how true was that fear? As he stumbled across the field with his captors, was there not something deeper inside him, something quite jaunty, that said, 'Never mind, nothing can touch you, this is just another adventure'?

Nothing can touch you, there is nothing you are not capable of. Those are the two things about him, two things that are really one thing, the thing that is right about him and the thing that is wrong about him at the same time. This thing that is two things means that he will not die, no matter what; but does it not also mean that he will not live?

He is a baby. His mother picks him up, face forward, gripping him under the arms. His legs hang, his head sags, he is naked; but his mother holds him up before her, advancing into the world. She has no need to see where she is going, she need only follow. Before him, as she advances, everything turns to stone and shatters. He is just a baby with a big belly and a lolling head, but he possesses this power.

Then he is asleep.

FOURTEEN

THERE IS A TELEPHONE CALL from Cape Town. Aunt Annie has had a fall on the steps of her flat in Rosebank. She has been taken to hospital with a broken hip; someone must come and make arrangements for her.

It is July, mid-winter. Over the whole of the Western Cape there is a blanket of cold and rain. They catch the morning train to Cape Town, he and his mother and his brother, then a bus up Kloof Street to the Volkshospitaal. Aunt Annie, tiny as a baby in her flowered nightdress, is in the female ward. The ward is full: old women with cross, pinched faces shuffling about in their dressing-gowns, hissing to themselves; fat, blowsy women with vacant faces sitting on the edges of their beds, their breasts carelessly spilling out. A loudspeaker in the corner plays Springbok Radio. Three o'clock, the afternoon request programme: 'When Irish Eyes are Smiling' with Nelson Riddle and his orchestra.

Aunt Annie takes his mother's arm in a wizened grip. 'I want to leave this place, Vera,' she says in her hoarse whisper. 'It is not the place for me.'

His mother pats her hand, tries to soothe her. On the bedside table, a glass of water for her teeth, and a Bible.

The ward sister tells them that the broken hip has been set.

Aunt Annie will have to spend another month in bed while the bone knits. 'She's not young any more, it takes time.' After that she will have to use a crutch.

As an afterthought the sister adds that when Aunt Annie was brought in her toenails were as long and black as birdclaws.

His brother, bored, has begun to whine, complaining he is thirsty. His mother stops a nurse and persuades her to fetch a glass of water. Embarrassed, he looks away.

They are sent down the corridor to the social worker's office. 'Are you the relatives?' says the social worker. 'Can you offer her a home?'

His mother's lips tighten. She shakes her head.

'Why can't she go back to her flat?' he says to his mother afterwards.

'She can't climb the stairs. She can't get to the shops.'

'I don't want her to live with us.'

'She is not coming to live with us.'

The visiting-hour is over, it is time to say goodbye. Tears well up in Aunt Annie's eyes. She clutches his mother's arm so tightly that her fingers have to be prised loose.

'*Ek wil huistoe gaan, Vera,*' she whispers—I want to go home.

'Just a few days more, Aunt Annie, till you can walk again,' says his mother in her most soothing voice.

He has never seen this side of her before: this treacherousness.

Then it is his turn. Aunt Annie reaches out a hand. Aunt Annie is both his great-aunt and his godmother. In the album there is a photograph of her with a baby in her arms said to be him. She is wearing a black dress down to her ankles and an old-fashioned black hat; there is a church in the background. Because she is his godmother she believes she has a special relationship with him. She does not seem to sense the disgust he feels for her, wrinkled and ugly in her hospital bed, the disgust he feels for this whole ward full of ugly women. He tries to keep his disgust from showing; his heart burns with shame. He endures the hand on his arm, but he wants to be gone, to be out of this place and never to come back.

'You are so clever,' says Aunt Annie in the low, hoarse voice she has had ever since he can remember. 'You are a big man, your mother depends on you. You must love her and be a support for her and for your little brother too.'

A support for his mother? What nonsense. His mother is like a rock, like a stone column. It is not he who must be a support for her, it is she who must be a support for him! Why is Aunt Annie saying these things anyhow? She is pretending she is going to die when all she has is a broken hip.

He nods, tries to look serious and attentive and obedient while secretly he is only waiting for her to let go of him. She smiles the meaningful smile that is meant to be a sign of the special bond between her and Vera's firstborn, a bond he does not feel at all, does not acknowledge. Her eyes are flat, pale blue, washed out. She is eighty years old and nearly blind. Even with glasses she cannot read the Bible properly, only hold it on her lap and murmur the words to herself.

She relaxes her grip; he mumbles something and retreats.

His brother's turn. His brother submits to being kissed. 'Goodbye, dear Vera,' croaks Aunt Annie. *'Mag die Here jou seën, jou en die kinders'*—May the Lord bless you and the children.

It is five o'clock and beginning to get dark. In the unfamiliar bustle of the city rush-hour they catch a train to Rosebank. They are going to spend the night in Aunt Annie's flat: the prospect fills him with gloom.

Aunt Annie has no fridge. Her larder contains nothing but a few withered apples, a mouldy half-loaf of bread, a jar of fishpaste that his mother does not trust. She sends him out to the Indian shop; they have bread and jam and tea for supper.

The toilet bowl is brown with dirt. His stomach turns when he thinks of the old woman with the long black toenails squatting over it. He does not want to use it.

'Why have we got to stay here?' he asks. 'Why have we got to stay here?' echoes his brother. 'Because,' says his mother grimly.

Aunt Annie uses forty-watt bulbs to save electricity. In the dim yellow light of the bedroom his mother begins to pack Aunt Annie's clothes into cardboard boxes. He had never been into Aunt Annie's bedroom before. There are pictures on the walls, framed photographs of men and women with stiff, forbidding looks: Brechers, du Biels, his ancestors.

'Why can't she go and live with Uncle Albert?'

'Because Kitty can't look after two sick old people.'

'I don't want her to live with us.'

'She is not going to live with us.'

'Then where is she going to live?'

'We will find a home for her.'

'What do you mean, a home?'

'A home, a home, a home for old people.'

The only room in Aunt Annie's flat that he likes is the storeroom. The storeroom is piled to the ceiling with old newspapers and cartons. There are shelves full of books, all the same: a squat book in a red binding, printed on the thick, coarse paper used for Afrikaans books that looks like blotting-paper with flecks of chaff and fly-dirt trapped in it. The title on the spine is *Ewige Genesing*; on the front cover is the full title, *Deur 'n gevaarlike krankheid tot ewige genesing*, Through a Dangerous Malady to Eternal Healing. The book was written by his great-grandfather, Aunt Annie's father; to it—he has heard the story many times—she has devoted most of her life, first translating the manuscript from German into Afrikaans, then spending her savings to pay a printer in Stellenbosch to print hundreds of copies, and a binder to bind some of them, then touring the bookshops of Cape Town. When the bookshops could not be persuaded to sell the book, she trudged from door to door herself. The leftovers are on the shelves here in the storeroom; the boxes contain folded, unbound printed pages.

He has tried to read *Ewige Genesing*, but it is too boring. No sooner has Balthazar du Biel got under way with the story of his boyhood in Germany than he interrupts it with long reports of lights in the sky and voices speaking to him out of the heavens. The whole of the book seems to be like that: short bits about himself followed by long recountings of what the voices told him. He and his father have long-standing jokes about Aunt Annie and her father Balthazar du Biel. They intone the title of his book in the sententious, sing-song manner of a *predikant*, drawing out the vowels: *'Deur 'n gevaaaarlike krannnnkheid tot eeeewige geneeeeesing.'*

'Was Aunt Annie's father mad?' he asks his mother.

'Yes, I suppose he was mad.'

'Then why did she spend all her money printing his book?'

'She was surely afraid of him. He was a terrible old German, terribly cruel and autocratic. All his children were afraid of him.'

'But wasn't he already dead?'

'Yes, he was dead, but she surely had a sense of duty toward him.'

She does not want to criticize Aunt Annie and her sense of duty toward the mad old man.

The best thing in the storeroom is the book press. It is made of iron as heavy and solid as the wheel of a locomotive. He persuades his brother to lay his arms in the bed of the press; then he turns the great screw until his arms are pinned and he cannot escape. After which they change places and his brother does the same to him.

One or two more turns, he thinks, and the bones will be crushed. What is it that makes them forbear, both of them?

During their first months in Worcester they were invited to one of the farms that supplied fruit to Standard Canners. While the grown-ups drank tea, he and his brother roamed around the farmyard. There they came upon a mealie-grinding machine. He persuaded his brother to put his hand down the funnel where the mealie-pits were thrown in; then he turned the handle. For an instant, before he stopped, he could feel the fine bones of the fingers being crushed. His brother stood with his hand trapped in the machine, ashen with pain, a puzzled, inquiring look on his face.

Their hosts rushed them all to the hospital, where a doctor amputated half the middle finger of his brother's left hand. For a while he walked around with his hand bandaged and his arm in a sling; then he wore a little black leather pouch over the finger-stump. He was six years old. Though no one pretended his finger would grow back, he did not complain.

He has never apologized to his brother, nor has he ever been reproached with what he did. Nevertheless, the memory lies like a weight upon him, the memory of the soft resistance of flesh and bone, and then the grinding.

'At least you can be proud to have someone in your family who did something with his life, who left something behind him,' says his mother.

'You said he was a horrible old man. You said he was cruel.'

'Yes, but he did something with his life.'

In the photograph in Aunt Annie's bedroom Balthazar du Biel

has grim, staring eyes and a tight, harsh mouth. Beside him his wife looks tired and cross. Balthazar du Biel met her, the daughter of another missionary, when he came to South Africa to convert the heathen. Later, when he travelled to America to preach the gospel, he took her and their three children along. On a paddle-steamer on the Mississippi someone gave his daughter Annie an apple, which she brought to show him. He gave her a thrashing for having spoken to a stranger. These are the few facts he knows about Balthazar, plus what is contained in the clumsy red book of which there are many more copies in the world than the world wants.

Balthazar's three children are Annie, Louisa—his mother's mother—and Albert, who figures in the photographs in Aunt Annie's bedroom as a frightened-looking boy in a sailor suit. Now Albert is Uncle Albert, a bent old man with pulpy white flesh like a mushroom who trembles all the time and has to be supported as he walks. Uncle Albert has never earned a proper salary in his life. He has spent his days writing books and stories; his wife has been the one to go out and work.

He asks his mother about Uncle Albert's books. She read one long ago, she says, but cannot remember it. 'They are very old-fashioned. People don't read books like that any more.'

He finds two books by Uncle Albert in the storeroom, printed on the same thick paper as *Ewige Genesing* but bound in brown covers, the same brown as benches on railways stations. One is called *Kain*, the other *Die Sondes van die vaders*, The Sins of the Fathers. 'Can I take them?' he asks his mother. 'I'm sure you can,' she says. 'No one is going to miss them.'

He tries to read *Die Sondes van die vaders*, but does not get beyond page ten, it is too boring.

'You must love your mother and be a support for her.' He

broods on Aunt Annie's instructions. *Love:* a word he mouths with distaste. Even his mother has learned not to say *I love you* to him, though now and then she slips in a soft *My love* when she says good-night.

He sees no sense in love. When men and women kiss in films, and violins play low and lush in the background, he squirms in his seat. He vows he will never be like that: soft, soppy.

He does not allow himself to be kissed, except by his father's sisters, making an exception for them because that is their custom and they can understand nothing else. Kissing is part of the price he pays for going to the farm: a quick brush of his lips against theirs, which are fortunately always dry. His mother's family does not kiss. Nor has he seen his mother and father kiss properly. Sometimes, when there are other people present and for some reason they have to pretend, his father kisses his mother on the cheek. She presents her cheek to him reluctantly, angrily, as if she were being forced; his kiss is light, quick, nervous.

He has seen his father's penis only once. That was in 1945, when his father had just come back from the War and all the family was gathered on Voëlfontein. His father and two of his brothers went hunting, taking him along. It was a hot day; arriving at a dam, they decided to swim. When he saw that they were going to swim naked, he tried to withdraw, but they would not let him. They were gay and full of jokes; they wanted him to take off his clothes and swim too, but he would not. So he saw all three penises, his father's most clearly of all, pale and white. He remembers clearly how he resented being made to look at it.

His parents sleep in separate beds. They have never had a double bed. The only double bed he has seen is on the farm, in the main bedroom, where his grandfather and grandmother used to sleep. He thinks of double beds as old-fashioned, belonging to the days when wives produced a baby a year, like ewes or sows. He is thankful his parents finished with that business before he knew about it.

He is prepared to believe that, long ago, in Victoria West, before he was born, his parents were in love, since love seems to be a precondition for marriage. There are photographs in the album that seem to prove it: the two of them sitting close together at a picnic, for instance. But all of that must have stopped years ago, and to his mind they are all the better for it.

As for him, what does the fierce and angry emotion he feels for his mother have to do with the deliquescent swooning on the screen? His mother loves him, that he acknowledges; but that is the problem, that is what is wrong, not what is right, with her attitude toward him. Her love emerges about all in her watchfulness, her readiness to pounce and save him should he ever be in danger. Should he choose (but he would never do so), he could relax into her care and for the rest of his life be borne by her. It is because he is so sure of her care that he is on his guard with her, never relaxing, never allowing her a chance.

He yearns to be rid of her watchful attention. There may come a time when to achieve this he will have to assert himself, refuse her so brutally that with a shock she will have to step back and release him. Yet he has only to think of that moment, imagine her surprised look, feel her hurt, and he is overtaken with a rush of guilt. Then he will do anything to soften the blow: console her, promise he is not going away.

Feeling her hurt, feeling it as intimately as if he were part of her, she part of him, he knows he is in a trap and cannot get out. Whose fault is it? He blames her, he is cross with her, but he is ashamed of his ingratitude too. *Love*: this is what love really is, this cage in which he rushes back and forth, back and forth, like a poor bewildered baboon. What can ignorant, innocent Aunt

Annie know about love? He knows a thousand times more about the world than she does, slaving her life away over her father's crazy manuscript. His heart is old, it is dark and hard, a heart of stone. That is his contemptible secret.

FIFTEEN

HIS MOTHER SPENT A YEAR at university before she had to make way for her younger brothers. His father is a qualified attorney; he works for Standard Canners only because to open a practice (so his mother tells him) would take more money than they have. Though he blames his parents because they have not brought him up as a normal child, he is proud of their education.

Because they speak English at home, because he always comes first in English at school, he thinks of himself as English. Though his surname is Afrikaans, though his father is more Afrikaans than English, though he himself speaks Afrikaans without any English accent, he could not pass for a moment as an Afrikaner. The range of Afrikaans he commands is thin and bodiless; there is a whole dense world of slang and allusion commanded by real Afrikaans boys—of which obscenity is only a part—to which he has no access.

There is a manner that Afrikaners have in common too—a surliness, an intransigence, and, not far behind it, a threat of physical force (he thinks of them as rhinoceroses, huge, lumbering, strong-sinewed, thudding against each other as they pass)—that he does not share and in fact shrinks from. They wield their language like a club against their enemies. On the streets it is best to avoid groups of them; even singly they have a truculent,

menacing air. Sometimes when the classes line up in the quadrangle in the mornings he scans the ranks of Afrikaans boys
looking for someone who is different, who has a touch of softness; but there is no one. It is unthinkable that he should ever
be cast among them: they would crush him, kill the spirit in him.

Yet, to his surprise, he finds himself unwilling to yield up the
Afrikaans language to them. He remembers his very first visit to
Voëlfontein, when he was four or five and could not speak
Afrikaans at all. His brother was still a baby, kept indoors out of
the sun; there was no one to play with but the Coloured children.
With them he made boats out of seed-pods and floated them
down the irrigation furrows. But he was like a mute creature:
everything had to be mimed; at times he felt he was going to
burst with the things he could not say. Then suddenly one day
he opened his mouth and found he could speak, speak easily
and fluently and without stopping to think. He still remembers
how he burst in on his mother, shouting 'Listen! I can speak
Afrikaans!'

When he speaks Afrikaans all the complications of life seem
suddenly to fall away. Afrikaans is like a ghostly envelope that
accompanies him everywhere, that he is free to slip into, becoming at once another person, simpler, gayer, lighter in his tread.

One thing about the English that disappoints him, that he will
not imitate, is their contempt for Afrikaans. When they lift their
eyebrows and superciliously mispronounce Afrikaans words, as
if *veld* spoken with a *v* were the sign of a gentleman, he draws
back from them: they are wrong, and, worse than wrong, comi-
cal. For his part, he makes no concessions, even among the English: he brings out the Afrikaans words as they ought to be
brought out, with all their hard consonants and difficult vowels.

It his class there are several boys besides himself with
Afrikaans surnames. In the Afrikaans classes, on the other

hand, there are no boys with English surnames. In the senior school he knows of one Afrikaans Smith who might as well be a Smit; that is all. It is a pity, but understandable: what Englishman would want to marry an Afrikaans woman and have an Afrikaans family when Afrikaans women are either huge and fat, with puffed-out breasts and bullfrog necks, or bony and misshapen?

He thanks God that his mother speaks English. But he remains mistrustful of his father, despite Shakespeare and Wordsworth and the *Cape Times* crossword puzzle. He does not see why his father goes on making the effort to be English here in Worcester, where it would be so easy for him to slide back into being Afrikaans. The childhood in Prince Albert that he hears his father joking about with his brothers strikes him as no different from an Afrikaans life in Worcester. It centres just as much on being beaten and on nakedness, on body functions performed in front of other boys, on an animal indifference to privacy.

The thought of being turned into an Afrikaans boy, with shaven head and no shoes, makes him quail. It is like being sent to prison, to a life without privacy. He cannot live without privacy. If he were Afrikaans he would have to live every minute of every day and night in the company of others. It is a prospect he cannot bear.

He remembers the three days of the Scout camp, remembers his misery, his craving, continually thwarted, to sneak back to the tent and read a book by himself.

One Saturday his father sends him to buy cigarettes. He has a choice between cycling all the way to the town centre, where there are proper shops with display windows and cash registers, and going to the little Afrikaans shop near the railway crossing, which is just a room at the back of a house with a counter painted dark brown and almost nothing on the shelves. He chooses the nearer.

It is a hot afternoon. In the shop there are strips of *biltong* hanging from the ceiling, and flies everywhere. He is about to tell the boy behind the counter—an Afrikaans boy older than himself—that he wants twenty Springbok plain when a fly flies into his mouth. He spits it out in disgust. The fly lies on the counter before him, struggling in a pool of saliva.

'*Sies!*' says one of the other customers.

He wants to protest: 'What must I do? Must I not spit? Must I swallow the fly? I am just a child!' But explanations count for nothing among these merciless people. He wipes the spit off the counter with his hand and amid disapproving silence pays for the cigarettes.

REMINISCING ABOUT THE OLD DAYS on the farm, his father and his father's brothers come once again to the subject of their own father. ' *'n Ware ou jintlman!*' they say, a real old gentleman, repeating their formula for him, and laugh: '*Dis wat hy op sy graf-steen sou gewens het:* A farmer and a gentleman'—That's what he would have liked on his gravestone. They laugh most of all because their father continued to wear riding boots when everyone else on the farm wore *velskoen*.

His mother, listening to them, sniffs scornfully. 'Don't forget how frightened you were of him,' she says. 'You were afraid to light a cigarette in front of him, even when you were grown men.'

They are abashed, they have no reply: she has clearly touched a nerve.

His grandfather, the one with the gentlemanly pretensions,

once owned not only the farm and a half-share in the hotel and general dealer's store at Fraserburg Road, but a house in Merweville with a flagpole in front of it on which he hoisted the Union Jack on the King's birthday.

' *'n Ware ou jintlman en 'n ware ou jingo!'* add the brothers: a real old jingo! Again they laugh.

His mother is right about them. They sound like children saying naughty words behind a parent's back. Anyway, by what right do they make fun of their father? But for him they would not speak English at all: they would be like their neighbours the Botes and the Nigrinis, stupid and heavy, with no conversation except about sheep and the weather. At least when the family gets together there is a babble of jokes and laughter in a mish-mash of tongues; whereas when the Nigrinis or the Botes come visiting the air at once turns sombre and heavy and dull. *'Ja-nee,'* say the Botes, sighing. *'Ja-nee,'* say the Coetzees, and pray that their guests will hurry up and leave.

What of himself? If the grandfather he reveres was a jingo, is he a jingo too? Can a child be a jingo? He stands to attention when *God Save the King* is played in the bioscope and the Union Jack waves on the screen. Bagpipe music sends a shiver down his spine, as do words like *stalwart, valorous*. Should he keep it a secret, this attachment of his to England?

He cannot understand why it is that so many people around him dislike England. England is Dunkirk and the Battle of Britain. England is doing one's duty and accepting one's fate in a quiet, unfussy way. England is the boy at the battle of Jutland, who stood by his guns while the deck was burning under him. England is Sir Lancelot of the Lake and Richard the Lionheart and Robin Hood with his longbow of yew and his suit of Lincoln green. What do the Afrikaners have to compare? Dirkie Uys, who rode his horse till it died. Piet Retief, who was made a fool of by Dingaan. And then the Voortrekkers getting their revenge by shooting thousands of Zulus who didn't have guns, and being proud of it.

There is a Church-of-England church in Worcester, and a clergyman with grey hair and a pipe who doubles as Scoutmaster and whom some of the English boys in his class—the proper English boys, with English names and homes in the old, leafy part of Worcester—refer to familiarly as Padre. When the English talk like that he falls silent. There is the English language, which he commands with ease. There is England and everything that England stands for, to which he believes he is loyal. But more than that is required, clearly, before one will be accepted as truly English: tests to face, some of which he knows he will not pass.

SIXTEEN

SOMETHING HAS BEEN ARRANGED on the telephone, he does not know what, but it makes him uneasy. He does not like the pleased, secretive smile his mother wears, the smile that means she had been meddling in his affairs.

These are the last days before they leave Worcester. They are also the best days of the school year, with examinations over and nothing to do but help the teacher fill in his mark book.

Mr Gouws reads out lists of marks; the boys add them up, subject by subject, then work out the percentages, racing to be the first with his hand up. The game lies in guessing which marks belong to whom. Usually he can recognize his own marks as a sequence rising to nineties and hundreds for arithmetic and tailing off with seventies for history and geography.

He does not do well at history or geography because he hates memorizing. So much does he hate it that he postpones learning for history and geography examinations until the last minute, until the night before the examination or even the morning of the examination. He hates the very sight of the history textbook, with its stiff chocolate-brown covers and its long, boring lists of the causes of things (the causes of the Napoleonic Wars, the causes of the Great Trek). Its authors are Taljaard and Schoeman. He imagines Taljaard as thin and dry, Schoeman as plump and balding and bespectacled; Taljaard and Schoeman sit across a table from each other in a room in Paarl, writing bad-tempered pages and passing them across to each other. He cannot imagine why they should have wanted to write their book in English except to teach the *Engelse* children a lesson.

Geography is no better—lists of towns, lists of rivers, lists of products. When he is asked to name the products of a country he always ends his list with hides and skins and hopes he is right. He does not know the difference between a hide and a skin, nor does anyone else.

As for the rest of the examinations, he does not look forward to them, yet, when the time comes, plunges into them willingly. He is good at examinations; if there were no examinations for him to be good at there would be little special about him. Examinations create in him a heady, trembling state of excitement during which he writes quickly and confidently. He does not like the state in itself but it is reassuring to know it is there to be tapped.

Sometimes, striking two rocks against each other and inhaling, he can reinvoke this state, this smell, this taste: gunpowder, iron, heat, a steady thudding in the veins.

The secret behind the telephone call, and behind his mother's smile, is revealed at the mid-morning break, when Mr Gouws motions him to stay behind. There is a false air about Mr Gouws, a friendliness he mistrusts.

Mr Gouws wants him to come to tea at his home. Dumbly he nods and memorizes the address.

This is not something he wants. Not that he dislikes Mr Gouws. If he does not trust him as much as he trusted Mrs Sanderson in Standard Four, that is only because Mr Gouws is a man, the first male teacher he has had, and he is wary of something that breathes from all men: a restlessness, a roughness barely curbed, a hint of pleasure in cruelty. He does not know how to behave toward Mr Gouws or toward men: whether to offer them no resistance and court their approval, or to maintain a barrier of stiffness. Women are easier because they are kinder. But Mr Gouws—he cannot deny it—is as fair as a person can be. His command of English is good, and he seems to bear no grudge against the English or against boys from Afrikaans families who prefer to be English. During one of his many absences from school, Mr Gouws taught the parsing of complements-of-the-predicate. He has trouble catching up with the class on complements-of-the-predicate. If complements-of-the-predicate made no sense, like idioms, then the other boys would also be having trouble with them. But the other boys, or most of them, seem to have a perfectly easy command of complements-of-the-predicate. The conclusion cannot be escaped: Mr Gouws knows something about English grammar that he does not.

Mr Gouws uses the cane as much as any other teacher. But his favourite punishment, when the class has been too noisy for too long, is to order them to put down their pens, shut their books, clasp their hands behind their heads, close their eyes, and sit absolutely still.

Save for Mr Gouws's footfalls as he patrols up and down the rows, there is absolute silence in the room. From the eucalyptus trees around the quadrangle comes the tranquil cooing of doves. This is a punishment he could endure forever, with equanimity: the doves, the soft breathing of the boys around him.

Disa Road, where Mr Gouws lives, is also in Reunion Park, in the new, northern extension of the township which he has never explored. Not only does Mr Gouws live in Reunion Park and cycle to school on a bicycle with fat tyres: he has a wife, a plain, dark woman, and, even more surprising, two small children. This he discovers in the living-room of 11 Disa Road, where there are scones and a pot of tea waiting on the table, and where, as he had feared, he is left alone with Mr Gouws, having to make desperate, false conversation.

It gets even worse. Mr Gouws—who has put aside his tie and jacket for shorts and khaki socks—is trying to pretend to him that, now that the school year is over, now that he is about to leave Worcester, the two of them can be friends. In fact he is trying to suggest that they have been friends all year: the teacher and the cleverest boy, the class leader.

He grows flustered and stiff. Mr Gouws offers him a second scone, which he refuses. 'Come on!' says Mr Gouws, and smiles, and puts it on his plate anyway. He longs to be gone.

He had wanted to leave Worcester with everything in order. He had been prepared to give Mr Gouws a place in his memory beside Mrs Sanderson: not quite with her, but close to her. Now Mr Gouws is spoiling it. He wishes he wouldn't.

The second scone sits on the plate uneaten. He will pretend no more: he grows mute and stubborn. 'Must you go?' says Mr Gouws. He nods. Mr Gouws rises and accompanies him to the front gate, which is a copy of the gate at 12 Poplar Avenue, the hinges whining on exactly the same high note.

At least Mr Gouws has the sense not to make him shake hands or do something else stupid.

THE DECISION TO LEAVE WORCESTER involves Standard Canners. His father has decided that his future does not lie with Standard Canners, which, according to him, is on its way down. He is going to return to legal practice.

There is a farewell party at the office from which his father returns with a new watch. Shortly thereafter he sets off for Cape Town, alone, leaving his mother behind to supervise the moving.

She hires a contractor named Retief, striking a bargain with him that for fifteen pounds he will convey not only the furniture but the three of them as well, in his cab.

Retief's men load the van, his mother and brother climb aboard. He makes a last dash around the empty house, saying goodbye. Behind the front door is the umbrella stand that usually holds two golf clubs and a walking stick, empty. 'They've left the umbrella stand!' he shouts. 'Come!' calls his mother— 'Forget that old umbrella stand!' 'No!' he shouts back, and will not leave until the men have fetched the umbrella stand. *'Dis net 'n ou stuk pyp,'* grumbles Retief—It's just an old piece of pipe.

So he learns that what he thought was an umbrella stand is nothing but a length of concrete sewer-pipe that his mother has brought indoors and painted green. This is what they are taking with them to Cape Town, along with the cushion covered in dog-hairs that Cossack used to sleep on, and the rolled-up netting-wire from the chicken-coop, and the machine that throws cricket balls, and the wooden stave with the Morse code. Labouring up Bain's Kloof Pass, Retief's van feels like Noah's Ark, saving the sticks and stones of their old life.

IN REUNION PARK they had paid twelve pounds a month for their house. The house his father has rented in Plumstead costs twenty-five pounds. It lies at the very limit of Plumstead, facing an expanse of sand and wattle bush where only a week after their arrival the police find a dead baby in a brown paper packet. A half-hour walk in the other direction lies Plumstead railway station. The house itself is newly built, like all the houses in Evremonde Road, with picture windows and parquet floors. The doors are warped, the locks do not lock, there is a pile of rubble in the back yard.

Next door live a couple newly arrived from England. The man is forever washing his car; the woman, wearing red shorts and sunglasses, spends her days in a deckchair, tanning her long white legs.

The immediate task is to find schools for him and his brother. Cape Town is not like Worcester, where all the boys went to the boys' school and all the girls to the girls' school. In Cape Town there are schools to choose among. But to get into a good school you need contacts, and they have few contacts.

Through the influence of his mother's brother Lance they get an interview at Rondebosch Boys' High. Dressed neatly in his shorts and shirt and tie and navy-blue blazer with the Worcester Boys' Primary badge on the breast pocket, he sits with his mother on a bench outside the headmaster's office. When their turn comes they are ushered into a wood-panelled room full of photographs of rugby and cricket teams. The headmaster's questions are all addressed to his mother: where they live, what his father does. Then comes the moment he has been waiting for. From her handbag she produces the report that proves he was first in class and that ought therefore to open all doors to him.

The headmaster puts on his reading-glasses. 'So you came first in your class,' he says. 'Good, good! But you won't find it so easy here.'

He had hoped to be tested: to be asked the date of the battle of Blood River, or, even better, to be given some mental arithmetic. But that is all, the interview is over. 'I can make no promises,' says the headmaster. 'His name will go down on the waiting-list, then we must hope for a withdrawal.'

His name goes down on the waiting-lists of three schools, without success. Coming first in Worcester is evidently not good enough for Cape Town.

The last resort is the Catholic school, St Joseph's. St Joseph's has no waiting-list: they will take anyone prepared to pay their fees, which for non-Catholics are twelve pounds a quarter.

What is being brought home to them, to him and his mother, is that in Cape Town different classes of people attend different schools. St Joseph's caters for, if not the lowest class, then the second-lowest. Her failure to get him into a better school leaves his mother bitter but does not upset him. He is not sure what class they belong to, where they fit in. For the present he is content merely to get by. The threat of being sent to an Afrikaans school and consigned to an Afrikaans life has receded—that is all that matters. He can relax. He does not even have to go on pretending to be a Catholic.

The real English do not go to a school like St Joseph's. But on the streets of Rondebosch, on their way to and from their own schools, he can see them every day, can admire their straight blond hair and golden skins, their clothes that are never too small or too large, their quiet confidence. They josh each other (a word he knows from the public-school stories he has read) in an easy way, without the raucousness and clumsiness he is used to. He has no aspiration to join them, but he watches and tries to learn.

The boys from Diocesan College, who are the most English of all and do not condescend even to play rugby or cricket against St Joseph's, live in select areas that, being far from the railway line, he hears of but never sees: Bishopscourt, Fernwood, Constantia. They have sisters who go to schools like Herschel and St Cyprian's, whom they genially watch over and protect. In Worcester he had rarely laid eyes on a girl: his friends seemed always to have brothers, not sisters. Now he glimpses for the first time the sisters of the English, so golden-blonde, so beautiful, that he cannot believe they are of this earth.

• • •

TO BE IN TIME FOR SCHOOL at 8.30 he needs to leave home by 7.30: a half-hour walk to the station, a fifteen-minute ride in the train, a five-minute walk from station to school, and a ten-minute cushion in case of delays. However, because he is frightened of being late, he leaves home at 7.00 and is at school by 8.00. There, in the classroom just unlocked by the janitor, he can sit at his desk with his head on his arms and wait.

He has nightmares of misreading his watchface, missing trains, taking wrong turns. In his nightmares he weeps in helpless despair.

The only boys who get to school before him are the De Freitas brothers, whose father, a greengrocer, drops them off at the crack of dawn from his battered blue truck, on his way to the Salt River produce market.

The teachers at St Joseph's belong to the Marist order. To him these Brothers, in their severe black cassocks and white starched stocks, are special people. Their air of mystery impresses him: the mystery of where they come from, the mystery of the names they have cast off. He does not like it when Brother Augustine, the cricket coach, comes to practice wearing a white shirt and black trousers and cricket boots like an ordinary person. He particularly does not like it when Brother Augustine, taking a turn to bat, slips a protector, a 'box,' under his trousers.

He does not know what the Brothers do when they are not teaching. The wing of the school building where they sleep and eat and live their private lives is off limits; he has no wish to penetrate it. He would like to think they live austere lives there, rising at four in the morning, spending hours in prayer, eating frugally, darning their own socks. When they behave badly, he does his best to excuse them. When Brother Alexis, for instance, who is fat and unshaven, breaks wind uncouthly and falls asleep in the Afrikaans class, he explains it to himself by saying that

Brother Alexis is an intelligent man who finds teaching beneath him. When Brother Jean-Pierre is suddenly transferred from duty in the junior dormitory amid stories that he has been doing things to small boys, he simply puts the stories out of his mind. It is inconceivable to him that Brothers should have sexual desires and not withstand them.

Since few of the Brothers speak English as a first language, they have hired a Catholic layman to take the English classes. Mr Whelan is Irish: he hates the English and barely conceals his dislike of Protestants. He also makes no effort to pronounce Afrikaans names correctly, speaking them with lips distastefully pursed as though they were heathen gibberish.

Most of their time in English classes is spent on Shakespeare's *Julius Caesar*, where Mr Whelan's method is to assign the boys roles and have them read their parts aloud. They also do exercises out of the grammar textbook and, once a week, write an essay. They have thirty minutes to write the essay before handing it in; in the remaining ten minutes Mr Whelan reads and marks all the essays, since he does not believe in taking work home. His ten-minute marking sessions have become one of his *pièces de résistance,* which the boys watch with admiring smiles. Blue pencil poised, Mr Whelan skims through the piles of essays. When at the end of his performance he shuffles the essay-books together and passes them to the class monitor to hand out, there is a subdued, ironic ripple of applause.

Mr Whelan's first name is Terence. He wears a brown leather motoring jacket and a hat. When it is cold he keeps his hat on, even indoors. He rubs his pale white hands together to warm them; he has the bloodless face of a corpse. What he is doing in South Africa, why he is not in Ireland, is not clear. He seems to disapprove of the country and everything that happens in it.

For Mr Whelan he writes essays on The Character of Mark

Antony, on The Character of Brutus, on Road Safety, on Sport, on Nature. Most of his essays are dull, mechanical performances; but occasionally he feels a spurt of excitement as he writes, and the pen begins to fly over the page. In one of his essays a high-wayman waits under cover at the roadside. His horse snorts softly, its breath turns to vapour in the cold night air. A ray of moonlight falls like a slash across his face; he holds his pistol under the flap of his coat to keep the powder dry.

The highwayman makes no impression on Mr Whelan. Mr Whelan's pale eyes flicker across the page, his pencil comes down: $6^1/_2$. $6^1/_2$ is the mark he almost always gets for his essays; never more than 7. Boys with English names get $7^1/_2$ or 8. Despite his funny surname, a boy named Theo Stavropoulos gets 8, because he dresses well and takes elocution lessons. Theo is also always allotted the part of Mark Antony, which means that he gets to read out 'Friends, Romans, countrymen, lend me your ears,' the most famous speech in the play.

In Worcester he had gone to school in a state of apprehension but of excitement too. True, he might at any time be exposed as a liar, with terrible consequences. Yet school was fascinating: each day seemed to bring new revelations of the cruelty and pain and hatred raging beneath the everyday surface of things. What was going on was wrong, he knew, should not be allowed to happen; and he was too young, too babyish and vulnerable, for what he was being exposed to. Nevertheless, the passion and fury of those days gripped him; he was shocked but he was greedy too to see more, to see all there was to see.

In Cape Town, in contrast, he soon feels he is wasting his time. School is no longer a place where great passions are aired. It is a shrunken little world, a more or less benign prison in which he might as well be weaving baskets as going through the classroom routine. Cape Town is not making him cleverer, it is making him stupider. The realization causes panic to well up in him. Whoever he truly is, whoever the true 'I' is that ought to be rising out of the ashes of his childhood, is not being allowed to be born, is being kept puny and stunted.

He has this feeling most despairingly in Mr Whelan's classes. There is a great deal more that he can write than Mr Whelan will ever allow. Writing for Mr Whelan is not like stretching his wings; on the contrary, it is like huddling in a ball, making himself as small and inoffensive as he can.

He has no wish to write about sport *(mens sana in corpore sano)* or road safety, which are so boring that he has to force out the words. He does not even want to write about highwaymen: he has a sense that the slivers of moonlight that fall across their faces and the white knuckles that grip their pistol-butts, whatever momentary impression they may make, are not his own, come from somewhere else and are already wilted. What he would write if he could, if it were not Mr Whelan reading it, would be something darker, something that, once it began to flow from his pen, would spread across the page out of control, like spilt ink. Like spilt ink, like shadows racing across the face of still water, like lightning crackling across the sky.

To Mr Whelan is also allotted the task of keeping the non-Catholic boys of Standard Six busy while the Catholic boys are in catechism class. He is supposed to read the Gospel of St Luke with them. Instead they hear over and over again about Parnell and Roger Casement and the perfidy of the English. But some days Mr Whelan comes to class with *Cape Times* in hand, boiling with rage at the newest outrages of the Russians in their satellite countries. 'In their schools they have created classes in atheism where children are forced to spit on the cross,' he thunders. 'Those who remain true to their faith are sent to infamous prison camps. That is the reality of Communism, which has the impudence to call itself the religion of Man.'

From Brother Otto they hear about the persecution of Christians in China. Brother Otto is not like Mr Whelan: he is quiet, blushes easily, has to be coaxed into telling stories. But his stories have more authority because he has actually been in China. 'Yes, I have seen it with my own eyes,' he says in his stumbling English: 'people in a tiny cell, locked up, so many that they could not breathe any more, and died. I have seen it.'

Ching-Chong-Chinaman, the boys call Brother Otto behind his back. To them, what Brother Otto tells about China or Mr Whelan about Russia is no more real than Jan van Riebeeck or the Great Trek. In fact, since Jan van Riebeeck and the Trek are on the Standard Six syllabus while Communism is not, what goes on in China and Russia can be ignored. China and Russia are just excuses to get Brother Otto or Mr Whelan talking.

As for him, he is troubled. He knows that his teachers' stories must be lies, but he has no means of proving it. He is discontented about having to sit captive listening to them, but too canny to protest or even demur. He has read the *Cape Times*, knows what happens to fellow-travellers. He has no wish to be denounced and ostracized.

Though Mr Whelan is less than enthusiastic about teaching Scripture to the non-Catholics, he cannot entirely neglect the Gospels. 'Unto him that smiteth thee on the one cheek, offer also the other,' he reads from Luke. 'What does Jesus mean? Does he mean that we should refuse to stand up for ourselves? Does he mean that we should be namby-pambies? Of course not. But if a bully comes up to you spoiling for a fight, Jesus says: Don't be provoked. There are better ways of settling differences than by fisticuffs.

'Unto every one that hath shall be given; and from him that hath not, even that which he hath shall be taken away. What does Jesus mean? Does he mean that the only way to attain salvation is to give away all we have? No. If Jesus had meant us to walk around in rags, he would have said so. Jesus speaks in parables. He tells us that those of us who truly believe will be rewarded with heaven, while those who have no belief will suffer eternal punishment in hell.'

He wonders whether Mr Whelan checks with the Brothers—particularly with Brother Odilo, who is the bursar and collects the school fees—before preaching these doctrines to the non-Catholics. Mr Whelan, the lay teacher, clearly believes that non-Catholics are heathens, damned. The Brothers themselves, on the other hand, are quite tolerant.

His resistance to Mr Whelan's Scripture lessons runs deep. He is sure that Mr Whelan has no idea of what Jesus' parables really mean. Though he himself is an atheist and has always been one, he feels he understands Jesus better than Mr Whelan does. He does not like Jesus—Jesus flies into a rage too easily—but he is prepared to put up with him. At least Jesus did not pretend to be God, and died before he could become a father. That is Jesus' strength; that is how Jesus keeps his power.

But there is one part in Luke's gospel that he does not like to hear read. When they come to it, he grows rigid, blocks his ears. The women arrive at the sepulchre to anoint the body of Jesus. Jesus is not there. Instead, they find two angels. 'Why seek ye the living among the dead?' say the angels: 'He is not here but is risen.' If he were to unblock his ears and let the words come through to him, he knows, he would have to stand on his seat and shout in triumph. He would have to make a fool of himself forever.

He does not feel that Mr Whelan personally wishes him ill.

Nevertheless, the highest mark he ever gets in English examinations is 70. With 70 he cannot come first in English: more favoured boys beat him comfortably. Nor does he do well in history or geography, which bore him more than ever. It is only the high marks he scores in mathematics and Latin that bring him tenuously to the head of the list, ahead of Oliver Matter, the Swiss boy who was cleverest in the class until he arrived.

Now that, in Oliver, he has come up against a worthy opponent, his old vow always to take home a first-place report becomes a matter of grim private honour. Though he says nothing about it to his mother, he is preparing for the day he cannot face, the day when he will have to tell her he has come second.

Oliver Matter is a gentle, smiling, moon-faced boy who does not seem to mind coming second as much as he would. Every day he and Oliver vie with each other in the quick-answer contest that Brother Gabriel runs, lining the boys up, going up and down the line asking questions that have to be answered within five seconds, sending whoever misses an answer to the bottom of the line. By the end of the round it is always either he or Oliver who is at the head.

Then Oliver stops coming to school. After a month without explanation, Brother Gabriel makes an announcement. Oliver is in hospital, he has leukemia, everyone must pray for him. With bowed heads the boys pray. Since he does not believe in God, he does not pray, just moves his lips. He thinks: Everyone will think I want Oliver to die so that I can be first.

Oliver never comes back. He dies in hospital. The Catholic boys attend a special mass for the repose of his soul.

The threat has receded. He breathes more easily; but the old pleasure in coming first is spoiled.

SEVENTEEN

LIFE IN CAPE TOWN is less varied than life in Worcester used to be. During weekends, in particular, there is nothing to do but read the *Reader's Digest* or listen to the radio or knock a cricket ball around. He no longer rides his bicycle: there is nowhere to go in Plumstead, which is just miles of houses in every direction, and anyhow he has outgrown the Smiths, which is beginning to look like a child's bicycle.

Riding a bicycle around the streets has in fact begun to seem silly. Other things that used once to absorb him have lost their charm too: building Meccano models, collecting stamps. He can no longer understand why he wasted his time on them. He spends hours in the bathroom, examining himself in the mirror, not liking what he sees. He stops smiling, practises a scowl.

The only passion that has not abated is his passion for cricket. He knows no one who is as consumed by cricket as he is. He plays cricket at school, but that is never enough. The house in Plumstead has a slate-floored front stoep. Here he plays by himself, holding the bat in his left hand, throwing the ball against the wall with his right, striking it on the rebound, imagining he is on a field. Hour after hour he drives the ball against the wall. The neighbours complain to his mother about the noise, but he pays no heed.

He has pored over coaching books, knows the various shots by heart, can execute them with the correct footwork. But the truth is, he prefers his solitary game on the stoep to real cricket. The prospect of batting on a real pitch thrills him but fills him with fear too. He is particularly afraid of fast bowlers: afraid of being struck, afraid of the pain. When he plays real cricket he has to concentrate all his energies on not flinching, not giving himself away.

He hardly ever scores runs. If he is not bowled out at once he can sometimes bat for half an hour without scoring, irritating everyone, including his teammates. He seems to go into a trance of passivity in which it is enough, quite enough, to merely parry the ball. Looking back on these failures, he consoles himself with stories of test matches played on sticky wickets during which a solitary figure, usually a Yorkshireman, dogged, stoic, tight-lipped, bats through the innings, keeping his end up while all around him wickets are tumbling.

Opening the batting against Pinelands Under-13 one Friday afternoon, he finds himself facing a tall, gangly boy who, urged on by his team, bowls as fast and furiously as he can. The ball flies all over the place, evading him, sometimes evading even the wicketkeeper: he barely needs to use his bat.

In the third over a ball pitches on the clay outside the mat, rears up, and hits him on the temple. 'This is really too much!' he thinks to himself crossly: 'He has gone too far!' He is aware of the fielders looking at him oddly. He can still hear the impact of ball against bone: a dull crack, without echo. Then his mind goes blank and he falls.

He is lying at the side of the field. His face and hair are wet. He looks around for his bat but cannot see it.

'Lie and rest for a while,' says Brother Augustine. His voice is quite cheery. 'You took a knock.'

'I want to bat,' he mumbles, and sits up. It is the correct thing to say, he knows: it proves one isn't a coward. But he can't bat: he has lost his turn, someone else is already batting in his place.

He would have expected them to make more of it. He would have expected an outcry against the dangerous bowler. But the game is going on, and his team is doing quite well. 'Are you OK? Is it sore?' asks one of his teammates, then barely listens to his reply. He sits on the boundary watching the rest of the innings. Later he fields. He would like to have a headache; he would like to lose his vision, or faint, or do something else dramatic. But he feels fine. He touches his temple. There is a tender spot. He hopes it swells up and turns blue before tomorrow, to prove he was really hit.

Like everyone at school, he has also to play rugby. Even a boy named Shepherd whose left arm is withered with polio has to play. They are given team positions quite arbitrarily. He is assigned to play prop for the Under-13Bs. They play on Saturday mornings. It is always raining on Saturdays: cold and wet and miserable, he trudges around the sodden turf from scrum to scrum, getting pushed around by bigger boys. Because he is a prop, no one passes the ball to him, for which he is grateful, since he is frightened of being tackled. Anyhow, the ball, which is coated in horsefat to protect the leather, is too slippery to hold on to.

He would pretend to be sick on Saturdays were it not for the fact that the team would then have only fourteen men. Not turning up for a rugby match is much worse than not coming to school.

The Under-13Bs lose all their matches. The Under-13As too lose most of the time. In fact, most of the St Joseph's teams lose most of the time. He does not understand why the school plays rugby at all. The Brothers, who are Austrian or Irish, are certainly not behind it. On the few occasions when they come to watch, they seem bemused and don't understand what is going on.

IN HER BOTTOM DRAWER his mother keeps a book with a black cover called *Ideal Marriage*. It is about sex; he has known about it for years. One day he spirits it out of the drawer and takes it to school. It causes a flurry among his friends; he appears to be the only one whose parents have such a book.

Though it is a disappointment to read—the drawings of the organs look like diagrams in science books, and even in the section on postures there is nothing exciting (inserting the male organ into the vagina sounds like an enema)—the other boys pore avidly over it, clamour to borrow it.

During the chemistry class he leaves the book behind in his desk. When they return Brother Gabriel, who is usually quite cheery, wears a frosty, disapproving look. He is convinced Brother Gabriel has opened his desk and seen the book; his heart pounds as he waits for the announcement and the shame that will follow. The announcement does not come; but in every passing remark of Brother Gabriel's he finds a veiled reference to the evil that he, a non-Catholic, has imported into the school. Everything is spoiled between Brother Gabriel and himself. Bitterly he regrets bringing the book; he takes it home, returns it to the drawer, never looks at it again.

For a while he and his friends continue to gather in a corner of the sportsfield during the break to talk about sex. To these discussions he contributes bits and pieces he has picked up from the book. But these are evidently not interesting enough: soon the older boys begin to separate off for conversations of their own in which there are sudden drops of tone, whisperings, outbursts of guffawing. At the centre of these conversations is Billy Owens, who is fourteen and has a sister of sixteen and knows girls and owns a leather jacket which he wears to dances and has possibly even had sexual intercourse.

He makes friends with Theo Stavropoulos. There are rumours that Theo is a *moffie*, a queer, but he is not prepared to believe them. He likes the look of Theo, likes his fine skin and his high colouring and his impeccable haircuts and the suave way he wears his clothes. Even the school blazer, with its silly vertical stripes, looks good on him.

Theo's father owns a factory. What exactly the factory makes no one quite knows, but it has something to do with fish. The family lives in a big house in the richest part of Rondebosch. They have so much money that the boys would undoubtedly go to Diocesan College were it not for the fact that they are Greek. Because they are Greek and have a foreign name they have to go to St Joseph's, which, he now sees, is a kind of basket to catch boys who fit nowhere else.

He glimpses Theo's father only once: a tall, elegantly dressed man with dark glasses. He sees his mother more often. She is small and slim and dark; she smokes cigarettes and drives a blue Buick which is reputed to be the only car in Cape Town—perhaps in South Africa—with automatic gears. There is also an older sister so beautiful, so expensively educated, so marriageable, that she is not allowed to be exposed to the gaze of Theo's friends.

The Stavropoulos boys are brought to school in the mornings in the blue Buick, driven sometimes by their mother but more often by a chauffeur in black uniform and peaked cap. The Buick sweeps grandly into the school quadrangle, Theo and his brother descend, the Buick sweeps off. He cannot understand why Theo allows this. If he were in Theo's place he would ask to be dropped off a block away. But Theo takes the jokes and jeers with equanimity.

One day after school Theo invites him to his house. When they get there he finds they are expected to have lunch. So at three in the afternoon they sit down at the dining-table with silver cutlery and clean napkins and are served steak and chips by a steward in a white uniform who stands behind Theo's chair while they eat, waiting for orders.

He does his best to conceal his astonishment. He knows there are people who are waited on by servants; he did not realize that children could have servants too.

Then Theo's parents and sister go overseas—the sister, rumour has it, to be married off to an English baronet—and Theo and his brother become boarders. He expects Theo to be crushed by the experience: by the envy and malice of the other boarders, by the poor food, by the indignities of a life without privacy. He also expects Theo to have to submit to the same kind of haircut as everyone else. Yet somehow Theo manages to keep his hair elegantly styled; somehow, despite his name, despite being clumsy at sport, despite being thought to be a *moffie*, he maintains his suave smile, never complains, never allows himself to be humiliated.

Theo sits squashed against him in his desk, underneath the picture of Jesus opening his chest to reveal a glowing ruby heart. They are supposed to be revising the history lesson; in fact they have a little grammar-book in front of them from which Theo is teaching him Ancient Greek. Ancient Greek with Modern Greek pronunciation: he loves the eccentricity of it. *Aftós*, whispers Theo; *evdhemonía. Evdhemonía*, he whispers back.

Brother Gabriel pricks up his ears. 'What are you doing, Stavropoulos?' he demands.

'I'm teaching him Greek, Brother,' says Theo in his bland, confident way.

'Go and sit in your own desk.'

Theo smiles and strolls back to his own desk.

The Brothers do not like Theo. His arrogance annoys them; they share the prejudice of the boys against his money. The injustice of it all angers him; he would like to do battle for Theo.

EIGHTEEN

TO TIDE THEM OVER until his father's new law practice begins to bring in money, his mother returns to teaching. For the housework she hires a maid, a scrawny woman with hardly any teeth named Celia. Sometimes Celia brings along her younger sister for company. Coming home one afternoon, he finds the two of them sitting in the kitchen drinking tea. The younger sister, who is more attractive than Celia, gives him a smile. There is something in her smile that confuses him; he does not know where to look and retires to his room. He can hear them laughing and knows they are laughing at him.

Something is changing. He seems to be embarrassed all the time. He does not know where to direct his eyes, what to do with his hands, how to hold his body, what expression to wear on his face. Everyone is staring at him, judging him, finding him wanting. He feels like a crab pulled out of its shell, pink and wounded and obscene.

Once upon a time he used to be full of ideas, ideas for places to go to, things to talk about, things to do. He was always a step ahead of everyone: he was the leader, the others followed. Now the energy that he used to feel streaming out of him is gone. At the age of thirteen he is becoming surly, scowling, dark. He does not like this new, ugly self, he wants to be drawn out of it, but that is something he cannot do by himself. Yet who is there who will do it for him?

They visit his father's new office to see what it is like. The office is in Goodwood, which belongs to the string of Afrikaans suburbs Goodwood-Parow-Bellville. Its windows are painted dark green; over the green in gold lettering are the words PROKUREUR—Z COETZEE—ATTORNEY. The interior is gloomy, with heavy furniture upholstered in horsehair and red leather. The law books that have travelled around South Africa with them since his father last practised in 1937 have emerged from their boxes and are on the shelf. Idly he looks up Rape. Natives sometimes insert the male organ between the thighs of the woman without penetration, says a footnote. The practice falls under customary law. It does not constitute rape.

Is this the kind of thing they do in law courts, he wonders: argue about where the penis went?

His father's practice appears to be flourishing. He employs not only a typist but an articled clerk named Eksteen. To Eksteen he leaves the routine business of conveyancing and wills; his own efforts he devotes to the exciting court work of *getting people off.* Each day he comes home with new stories of people whom he has got off, and of how grateful they are to him.

His mother is less interested in the people he has got off than in the mounting list of monies owed. One name in particular keeps cropping up: Le Roux the car salesman. She badgers his father: he is a lawyer, surely he can get Le Roux to pay. Le Roux will settle his debt for sure at the end of the month, replies his father, he has promised. But at the end of the month, once again, Le Roux does not settle.

Le Roux does not settle, nor does he make himself scarce. On the contrary, he invites his father for drinks, promises him more work, paints rosy pictures of the money to be made from repossessing cars.

The arguments at home become angrier but at the same time more guarded. He asks his mother what is going on. Bitterly she says, Jack has been lending Le Roux money.

He does not need to hear more. He knows his father, knows what is going on. His father craves approval, will do anything to be liked. In the circles in which his father moves there are only two ways of getting to be liked: buying people drinks and lending them money.

Children are not supposed to go into bars. But in the bar of the Fraserburg Road hotel he and his brother have sat at a corner table, drinking orange squash, watching their father buy rounds of brandy and water for strangers, getting to know this other side of him. So he knows the mood of expansive bonhomie that brandy creates in him, the boasting, the large spendthrift gestures.

Avidly, gloomily, he listens to his mother's monologues of complaint. Though his father's wiles no longer take him in, he cannot trust her to resist them: he has seen his father wheedle his way past her too often in the past. 'Don't listen to him,' he warns her. 'He lies to you all the time.'

The trouble with Le Roux deepens. There are long telephone calls. A new name starts cropping up: Bensusan. Bensusan is dependable, says his mother. Bensusan is a Jew, he doesn't drink. Bensusan is going to rescue Jack, put him back on the right track.

But there is not only Le Roux, it turns out. There are other men, other drinking companions, to whom his father has been lending money. He cannot believe it, cannot understand it. Where does all this money come from, when his father has only one suit and one pair of shoes and has to catch the train to work? Does one really make so much money so quickly getting people off?

He has never seen Le Roux but can picture him easily enough. Le Roux will be a ruddy Afrikaner with a blond moustache; he will wear a blue suit and a black tie; he will be slightly fat and sweat a lot and tell dirty jokes in a loud voice.

Le Roux sits with his father in the bar in Goodwood. When his father isn't looking Le Roux winks behind his back to the other men in the bar. Le Roux has picked out his father as a sucker. He burns with shame that his father should be so stupid.

The money, it turns out, is not actually his father's. That is why Bensusan has involved himself. Bensusan is acting for the Law Society. The matter is serious: the money is from his father's trust account. 'What is a trust account?' he asks his mother. 'It's money he has on trust.' 'Why do people give him their money on trust?' he says. 'They must be mad.' His mother shakes her head. Attorneys have trust accounts, she says, God only knows why. 'Jack is like a child when it comes to money,' she says.

Bensusan and the Law Society have entered the picture because there are people who want to save his father, people from the old days when he was Controller of Letting, before the Nationalists took over. They are well disposed toward his father, they don't want him to go to jail. For old times' sake, and because he has a wife and children, they will close their eyes to certain things, make certain arrangements. He can make repayments over five years; then the book will be closed, the matter forgotten.

His mother takes legal advice herself. She would like her own possessions to be separated from her husband's before some new disaster strikes: the dining-room table, for instance; the chest of drawers with the mirror; the stinkwood coffee-table that Aunt Annie gave her. She would like their marriage contract, which makes the two of them responsible for each other's debts, to be amended. But marriage contracts, it turns out, are immutable. If his father goes down, his mother goes down too, she and her children.

Eksteen and the typist are given notice, the practice in Goodwood is closed. He never gets to see what happens to the green window with the gold lettering. His mother continues to teach. His father starts looking for a job. Every morning, punctually at seven, he sets off for the city. But an hour or two later—this is his secret—when everyone else has left the house, he comes back. He puts on his pyjamas again and gets into bed with the *Cape Times* crossword, a half-jack of brandy and a jug of water. At two in the afternoon, before the others return, he dresses and goes to his club.

The club is called the Wynberg Club, but it is really just part of the Wynberg Hotel. There his father has supper and spends the evening drinking. Sometime after midnight—the noise wakes him, he does not sleep heavily—a car pulls up before the house, the front door opens, his father comes in and goes to the lavatory. Then from his parents' bedroom comes a flurry of heated whispering. In the morning there are dark-yellow splashes on the lavatory floor and on the toilet seat, and a sickly-sweet smell.

He writes a notice and puts it in the lavatory: PLEASE LIFT THE SEAT. The notice is ignored. Urinating on the toilet seat becomes his father's last act of defiance against a wife and children who have stopped speaking to him.

He discovers his father's secret one day when he stays away from school, ill or pretending to be ill. From his bed he hears the scrape of the key in the front-door lock, hears his father settling down in the next room. Later, guilty, angry, they pass each other in the passage.

Before leaving the house in the afternoons his father empties the mailbox and removes certain letters, which he hides at the bottom of his wardrobe, under the paper lining. When at last the floodgates burst, it is the cache of letters in the wardrobe—bills from the Goodwood days, letters of demand, lawyers' letters—that his mother is most bitter about. 'If I had only known, I could have made a plan,' she says. 'Now everything is ruined.'

The debts stretch everywhere. Callers come at all hours of the day and night, callers whom he does not get to see. Each time there is a knock at the front door his father shuts himself up in his bedroom. His mother greets the visitors in low tones, ushers them into the living-room, closes the door. Afterwards he can hear her whispering angrily to herself in the kitchen.

There is talk of Alcoholics Anonymous, of how his father should go to Alcoholics Anonymous to prove his sincerity. His father promises but does not go.

Two court officers arrive to take an inventory of the contents of the house. It is a sunny Saturday morning. He retreats to his bedroom and tries to read, but it is no good: the men require access to his room, to every room. He goes into the back yard. Even there they follow him, glancing around, making notes on a pad.

He seethes with rage all the time. *That man*, he calls his father when he speaks to his mother, too full of hatred to give him a name: why do we have to have anything to do with *that man*? Why don't you let *that man* go to prison?

He has twenty-five pounds in his Post Office savings book. His mother swears to him that no one will take his twenty-five pounds.

There is a visit from a Mr Golding. Though Mr Golding is

Coloured, he is somehow in a position of power over his father. Careful preparations are made for the visit. Mr Golding will be received in the front room, like other callers. He will be served tea in the same tea service. In return for being treated so well, it is hoped that Mr Golding will not prosecute.

Mr Golding arrives. He wears a double-breasted suit, does not smile. He drinks the tea that his mother serves but will promise nothing. He wants his money.

After he has left there is a debate about what to do with the teacup. The custom, it appears, is that after a person of colour has drunk from a cup the cup must be smashed. He is surprised that his mother's family, which believes in nothing else, believes in this. However, in the end his mother simply washes the cup with bleach.

At the last minute Aunt Girlie from Williston comes to the rescue, for the honour of the family. She lays down certain conditions, one of them that Jack should never again practise as an attorney.

His father agrees to the conditions, agrees to sign the document. But when the time comes, it takes long cajoling to get him out of bed. At last he makes his appearance, in grey slacks and a pyjama top and bare feet. Wordlessly he signs; then he retires to his bed again.

Later that evening he gets dressed and goes out. Where he spends the night they do not know; he does not return until the next day.

'What's the point of making him sign?' he complains to his mother. 'He never pays his other debts, why should he pay Girlie?'

'Never mind him, I'll pay her,' she replies.

'How?'

'I'll work for it.'

There is something in her behaviour that he can no longer close his eyes to, something extraordinary. With each new revelation she seems to grow stronger and more stubborn. It is as though she is inviting calamities upon herself for no other purpose than to show the world how much she can endure. 'I will pay all his debts,' she says. 'I will pay in instalments. I will work.'

Her ant-like determination angers him to the point that he wants to strike her. It is clear what lies behind it. She wants to sacrifice herself for her children. Sacrifice without end: he is all too familiar with that spirit. But once she has sacrificed herself entirely, once she has sold the clothes off her back, sold her very shoes, and is walking around on bloody feet, where will that leave him? It is a thought he cannot bear.

THE DECEMBER HOLIDAYS ARRIVE and still his father has no job. They are all four in the house now, like rats in a cage, avoiding each other, hiding in separate rooms. His brother absorbs himself in comics: the *Eagle*, the *Beano*. His own favourite is the *Rover*, with its stories of Alf Tupper, the one-mile champion who works in a factory in Manchester and lives on fish and chips. He tries to forget himself, but he cannot help pricking his ears to every whisper and creak in the house.

One morning there is a strange silence. His mother is out, but from something in the air, a smell, an aura, a heaviness, he knows that *that man* is still here. Surely he cannot still be sleeping. Is it possible that, wonder of wonders, he has committed suicide?

But if he has committed suicide, would it not be best to pretend not to notice, so that the sleeping-pills or whatever he has taken can be given time to act? And how can he keep his brother from raising the alarm?

In the war he has waged on his father, he has never been entirely sure of his brother's support. As far back as he can remember, people have remarked that, whereas he takes after his mother, his brother has his father's looks. He suspects his brother may be soft on his father; he suspects his brother, with his pale, worried face and the tic on his eyelid, of being soft in general.

It would certainly be best to steer clear of *his* room, so that if there are questions afterwards, he will be able to say, 'I was talking to my brother,' or 'I was reading in my room.' But he cannot contain his curiosity. He tiptoes to the door, pushes it open, looks in.

It is a warm summer morning. The wind is still, so still that he can hear the chirruping of sparrows outside, the whirr of their wings. The shutters are closed, the curtains drawn shut. There is a smell of man's sweat. In the gloom he can make out his father lying on his bed. From the back of his throat comes a soft gargling as he breathes.

He steps closer. His eyes are growing accustomed to the light. His father is wearing pyjama pants and a cotton singlet. He has not shaved. There is a red V at his throat where sunburn gives way to the pallor of his chest. Beside the bed is a chamber-pot in which cigarette-stubs float in brownish urine. He has not seen anything uglier in his life.

There are no pills. The man is not dying, merely sleeping. He does not have the courage to take sleeping-pills, just as he does not have the courage to go out and look for a job.

Since the day his father came back from the War they have fought, in a second war which his father has stood no chance of winning because he could never have foreseen how pitiless, how tenacious his enemy would be. For seven years that war has ground on; today he has triumphed. He feels like the Russian soldier on the Brandenburg Gate, raising the red banner over the ruins of Berlin.

Yet at the same time he wishes he were not here, witnessing the shame. Unfair! he wants to cry: I am just a child! He wishes that someone, a woman, would take him in her arms, make his wounds better, soothe him, tell him it was just a bad dream. He thinks of his grandmother's cheek, soft and cool and dry as silk, offered to him to be kissed. He wishes his grandmother would come and put it all right.

A ball of phlegm catches in his father's throat. He coughs, turns on his side. His eyes open, the eyes of a man fully conscious, fully aware of where he is. The eyes take him in as he stands there, where he should not be, spying. The eyes are without judgment but without kindness either.

Lazily the man's hand sweeps down and rearranges his pyjama pants.

He would expect the man to say something, some word— 'What time is it?'—to make it easier for him. But the man says nothing. The eyes continue to regard him, peaceably, distantly. Then they close and he is asleep again.

He returns to his room, closes the door.

Sometimes the gloom lifts. The sky, that usually sits tight and closed over his head, not so near that it can be touched but not much further either, opens a slit, and for an interval he can see the world as it really is. He sees himself in his white shirt with rolled-up sleeves and the grey short trousers that he is on the point of outgrowing: not a child, not what a passer-by would call a child, too big for that now, too big to use that excuse, yet still as stupid and self-enclosed as a child: childish; dumb; ignorant;

retarded. In a moment like this he can see his father and his mother too, from above, without anger: not as two grey and form-less weights seating themselves on his shoulders, plotting his misery day and night, but as a man and a woman living dull and trouble-filled lives of their own. The sky opens, he sees the world as it is, then the sky closes and he is himself again, living the only story he will admit, the story of himself.

His mother stands at the sink, in the dimmest corner of the kitchen. She stands with her back to him, her arms flecked with soapsuds, scouring a pot, in no great hurry. As for him, he is roaming around, talking about something, he does not know what, talking with his usual vehemence, complaining.

She turns from her chore; her gaze flickers over him. It is a considered look, and without any fondness. She is not seeing him for the first time. Rather, she is seeing him as he has always been and as she has always known him to be when she is not wrapped up in illusion. She sees him, sums him up, and is not pleased. She is even bored with him.

This is what he fears from her, from the person in all the world who knows him best, who has the huge advantage over him of knowing all about his first, most helpless, most intimate years, years of which, despite every effort, he himself can re-member nothing; who probably knows as well, since she is in-quisitive and has sources of her own, the paltry secrets of his school life. He fears her judgment. He fears the cool thoughts that must be passing through her mind at moments like this, when there is no passion to colour them, no reason for her judg-ment to be anything but clear; above all he fears the moment, a moment that has not yet arrived, when she will utter her judg-ment. It will be like a stroke of lightning; he will not be able to withstand it. He does not want to know. So much does he not want to know that he can feel a hand go up inside his own head to block his ears, block his sight. He would rather be blind and deaf than know what she thinks of him. He would rather live like a tortoise inside its shell.

This woman was not brought into the world for the sole purpose of loving him and protecting him and taking care of his wants. On the contrary, she had a life before he came into being, a life in which there was no requirement upon her to give him the slightest thought. At a certain time in her life she bore him; she bore him and she decided to love him; perhaps she chose to love him even before she bore him; nevertheless, she chose to love him, and therefore she can choose to stop loving him.

'Wait until you have children of your own,' she says to him in one of her bitterer moods. 'Then you will know.' What will he know? It is a formula she uses, a formula that sounds as if it comes from the old days. Perhaps it is what each generation says to the next, as a warning, as a threat. But he does not want to hear it. 'Wait until you have children.' What nonsense, what a contradiction! How can a child have children? Anyway, what he would know if he were a father, if he were his own father, is precisely what he does not want to know. He will not accept the vision that she wants to force upon him: sober, disappointed, disillusioned.

NINETEEN

AUNT ANNIE IS DEAD. Despite the promises of the doctors, she never walked after her fall, not even with a stick. From her bed in the Volkshospitaal she was transferred to a bed in an old-age home in Stikland, in the back of beyond, where no one had the time to visit her and where she died alone. Now she is to be buried in Woltemade cemetery no. 3.

At first he refuses to go. He gets enough prayers at school, he says, he does not want to hear more. He is vocal in his scorn for the tears that are going to be shed. Giving Aunt Annie a proper funeral is just a way for her relatives to make themselves feel good. She should be buried in a hole in the garden of the old-age home. It would save money.

In his heart he does not mean it. But he needs to say things like this to his mother, needs to watch her face tighten in hurt and outrage. How much more must he say before she will at last round on him and tell him to be quiet?

He does not like to think of death. He would prefer it if, when people got old and sick, they simply stopped existing and disappeared. He does not like ugly old bodies; the thought of old people taking off their clothes makes him shudder. He hopes that the bath in their house in Plumstead has never had an old person in it.

His own death is a different matter. He is always somehow present after his death, floating above the spectacle, enjoying the grief of those who caused it and who, now that it is too late, wish he were still alive.

In the end, however, he does go with his mother to Aunt Annie's funeral. He goes because she pleads with him, and he likes being pleaded with, likes the feeling of power it gives; also because he has never been to a funeral and wants to see how deep they dig the grave, how a coffin is lowered into it.

It is not a grand funeral at all. There are only five mourners, and a young Dutch Reformed *dominee* with pimples. The five are Uncle Albert and his wife and son, and his mother and himself. He has not seen Uncle Albert for years. He is bent almost double over his stick; tears stream from his pale blue eyes; the wings of his collar stick out as though his tie has been knotted by other hands.

The hearse arrives. The undertaker and his assistant are in formal black, far more smartly dressed than any of them (he is in his St Joseph's school uniform: he has no suit). The *dominee* says a prayer in Afrikaans for the departed sister; then the hearse is reversed to the graveside and the coffin is slid out, onto poles over the grave. To his disappointment, it is not lowered into the grave—that must wait, it appears, for the graveyard workers—but discreetly the undertaker gestures that they may toss clods of earth on to it.

A light rain begins to fall. The business is over; they are free to go, free to return to their own lives.

On the path back to the gate, through acres of graves old and new, he walks behind his mother and her cousin, Albert's son, who are talking in low voices. They have the same plodding gait, he notices, the same way of lifting their legs and setting them down heavily, left then right, like peasants in clogs. The du Biels of Pomerania: peasants from the countryside, too slow and heavy for the city; out of place.

He thinks of Aunt Annie, whom they have abandoned here in the rain, in godforsaken Woltemade, thinks of the long black talons that the nurse in the hospital cut for her, that no one will cut any more.

'You know so much,' Aunt Annie once said to him. It was not praise: though her lips were pursed in a smile, she was shaking her head at the same time. 'So young and yet you know so much. How are you ever going to keep it all in your head?' And she leaned over and tapped his skull with a bony finger.

The boy is special, Aunt Annie told his mother, and his mother in turn told him. But what kind of special? No one ever says.

They have reached the gate. It is raining harder. Even before they can catch their two trains, the train to Salt River and then the train to Plumstead, they will have to trudge through the rain to Woltemade station.

The hearse passes them. His mother holds out a hand to stop it, speaks to the undertaker. 'They will give us a lift in to town,' she says.

So he has to climb into the hearse and sit crammed between his mother and the undertaker, cruising sedately down Voortrekker Road, hating her for it, hoping that no one from his school will see him.

'The lady was a schoolteacher, I believe,' says the undertaker. He speaks with a Scots accent. An immigrant: what can he know of South Africa, of people like Aunt Annie?

He has never seen a hairier man. Black hair sprouts from his nose and his ears, sticks out in tufts from his starched cuffs.

'Yes,' says his mother: 'she taught for over forty years.'

'Then she left some good behind,' says the undertaker. 'A noble profession, teaching.'

'What has happened to Aunt Annie's books?' he asks his mother later, when they are alone again. He says books, but he only means *Ewige Genesing* in its many copies.

His mother does not know or will not say. From the flat where she broke her hip to the hospital to the old age home in Stikland to Woltemade no. 3 no one has given a thought to the books except perhaps Aunt Annie herself, the books that no one will ever read; and now Aunt Annie is lying in the rain waiting for someone to find the time to bury her. He alone is left to do the thinking. How will he keep them all in his head, all the books, all the people, all the stories? And if he does not remember them, who will?

J. M. Coetzee is "South Africa's most brilliant novelist."
(Seattle Times)

☐ **BOYHOOD**
A memoir that is "fiercely revealing, bluntly unsentimental . . . a telling portrait of the artist as a young man that illuminates the hidden sources of his art."
—Michiko Kakutani, *The New York Times*   ISBN 0-14-026566-X

☐ **THE MASTER OF PETERSBURG**
"A fascinating study of the dark mysteries of creativity, grief, relationships between fathers and sons, and of the great Russian themes of love and death."
—*The Wall Street Journal*   ISBN 0-14-023810-7

☐ **AGE OF IRON**
"Coetzee is one of the greatest living writers of our time . . . *Age of Iron* is taut, ironic, grieving and, finally, astonishing." —*Los Angeles Times*
                    ISBN 0-14-027565-7

☐ **FOE**
"A finely honed testament to its author's intelligence, imagination, and skill. . . . The writing is lucid and precise, the landscape depicted mythic, yet specific."
—Michiko Kakutani, *The New York Times*   ISBN 0-14-009623-X

☐ **LIFE & TIMES OF MICHAEL K**
"An outstanding achievement." —Nadine Gordimer   ISBN 0-14-007448-1

☐ **WAITING FOR THE BARBARIANS**
"A real literary event."—Irving Howe, front page, *The New York Times Book Review*
                    ISBN 0-14-006110-X

☐ **IN THE HEART OF THE COUNTRY**
"A realistic fable, at once stark, exciting, and economical."
—*The New York Times Book Review*   ISBN 0-14-006228-9

☐ **DUSKLANDS**
"His writing gives off whiffs of Conrad, of Nabokov, of Golding, of the Paul Theroux of *The Mosquito Coast*. But he is none of these, he is a harsh, compelling new voice." —*Sunday Times*   ISBN 0-14-024177-9

FOR THE BEST IN PAPERBACKS, LOOK FOR THE

In every corner of the world, on every subject under the sun, Penguin represents quality and variety—the very best in publishing today.

For complete information about books available from Penguin—including Puffins, Penguin Classics, and Arkana—and how to order them, write to us at the appropriate address below. Please note that for copyright reasons the selection of books varies from country to country.

In the United Kingdom: Please write to *Dept. JC, Penguin Books Ltd, FREEPOST, West Drayton, Middlesex UB7 0BR.*

If you have any difficulty in obtaining a title, please send your order with the correct money, plus ten percent for postage and packaging, to *P.O. Box No. 11, West Drayton, Middlesex UB7 0BR*

In the United States: Please write to *Consumer Sales, Penguin USA, P.O. Box 999, Dept. 17109, Bergenfield, New Jersey 07621-0120.* VISA and MasterCard holders call 1-800-253-6476 to order all Penguin titles

In Canada: Please write to *Penguin Books Canada Ltd, 10 Alcorn Avenue, Suite 300, Toronto, Ontario M4V 3B2*

In Australia: Please write to *Penguin Books Australia Ltd, P.O. Box 257, Ringwood, Victoria 3134*

In New Zealand: Please write to *Penguin Books (NZ) Ltd, Private Bag 102902, North Shore Mail Centre, Auckland 10*

In India: Please write to *Penguin Books India Pvt Ltd, 706 Eros Apartments, 56 Nehru Place, New Delhi 110 019*

In the Netherlands: Please write to *Penguin Books Netherlands bv, Postbus 3507, NL-1001 AH Amsterdam*

In Germany: Please write to *Penguin Books Deutschland GmbH, Metzlerstrasse 26, 60594 Frankfurt am Main*

In Spain: Please write to *Penguin Books S. A., Bravo Murillo 19, 1° B, 28015 Madrid*

In Italy: Please write to *Penguin Italia s.r.l., Via Felice Casati 20, I-20124 Milano*

In France: Please write to *Penguin France S. A., 17 rue Lejeune, F–31000 Toulouse*

In Japan: Please write to *Penguin Books Japan, Ishikiribashi Building, 2–5–4, Suido, Bunkyo-ku, Tokyo 112*

In Greece: Please write to *Penguin Hellas Ltd, Dimocritou 3, GR–106 71 Athens*

In South Africa: Please write to *Longman Penguin Southern Africa (Pty) Ltd, Private Bag X08, Bertsham 2013*